SELF-LOVE SECRETS
How to Love Yourself
Unconditionally

By Evelyn Lim

SELF-LOVE SECRETS
WRITTEN BY EVELYN LIM

ACKNOWLEDGEMENTS

I wish to express thanks to the many readers of my blog,
who have written to me. There are far
too many of them for me to thank individually.
It was their emails that led to
the writing of this book.

Also, thanks to my clients, friends and family
who have helped provide the case studies contained within.

Each has also further assisted me with
greater insights into myself. The
self-knowledge gained has been priceless.

DEDICATION

I dedicate this book to my dear husband,
who also happens to be my soul mate.
I am blessed to have him as my companion in my
journey towards loving myself.
I thank him dearly for being there
for me at a time when I had to
navigate my way from darkness to light.

I also dedicate this book to my two girls,
who have taught me many invaluable lessons on
unconditional love and acceptance.
I have been a better person
because of them.

Loving all at home always.

"Beyond a wholesome discipline,
be gentle with yourself.
You are a child of the universe,
no less than the trees and the stars;
you have a right to be here.
And whether or not it is clear to you,
no doubt the universe is
unfolding as it should."
- Max Ehrmann (1872 - 1945)

Table of Contents

CHAPTER ONE:
A WORLD STARVED OF SELF-LOVE

"You must love yourself before you love another. By accepting yourself and fully being what you are, your simple presence can make others happy."
- Anonymous

Self-Love Anorexia

Self-love starvers are on an anorexic diet. They have little sustenance to thrive on. Their diet is strict and limiting, depriving the heart of needed love calories. Unfortunately, while the anorexic diet is applied at the heart, negative consequences are experienced throughout all levels; mind, body and spirit. As a result, self-love starvers find that every facet of their lives – home, relationship, work, friends, finance and so on - get affected.

Let's see if the following description of a self-love starver applies to you too. Deficient in love, your heart has been aching for the nourishment it needs. Yet, you have been unable to embrace yourself with compassion, you hate parts of how your body looks and you have got nothing kind to say towards the self. Consequently, you have not been able to function well.

There is a lack of warmth in your inner world. Your relationship with the self is as chilly as the winds in Siberia. And so your heart has been frozen from the inside. With not enough sustenance to go on, it has been difficult to feel alive. Your eyes reveal the emptiness of your soul. Invariably, you have also found that the lack of warmth on the inside is no different from that on the outside. You have been barely scraping by.

It is hard to muster a sense of excitement when you get up in the mornings. There have been days when you wake up with tremendous pain, from having spent the night on a bed of sharp pointed nails. If anything at all, you are great at inflicting injury inwards. Then again, walking around with gaping wounds is not such a big deal anymore because you have pretty much grown accustomed to your pain. Without a question, you have been slow in placing importance on your needs. Self-care is often placed at the bottom of your priority.

It is not as if you need to beg for love. Others have been hoping to send some your way. However, you simply refuse to receive any. The problem is that you deem yourself intrinsically unworthy to receive any. It has been hard to accept any compliments, gifts or notes of appreciation. You either do not believe the nice things that others say about you or you have been wired not to accept anything that you may feel indebted for.

You are aware of your soul-less existence but then again, it has been uphill trying to practice self-love. For a long time, the stories in your self-talk have been hijacking you. They have over-written every single dream you may have. Hope has been blacklisted as a welcome guest in your inner world. Limiting, crippling and destructive, your inner talk has left you depressed, drained and dispirited. For the most part, you feel depleted of energy.

Every decision that you make, from as little as what to wear this morning, to major ones like career choices and whether or not to pursue your dreams, is influenced by the voice inside your head. Your eye for perfection has meant that you are highly skilled in picking up flaws, mistakes and weaknesses. Thus, you have developed an obsessive tendency to focus on the parts that are "wrong", "imperfect", or "not good enough".

Drowned by the voice of your critic, you have not been able to tune into joy. You are inflicted with shame, rejection, anger, distrust, suspicion and jealousy. It is a heavy load of emotional baggage that you have been carrying everywhere. Consequently, you have been extremely unhappy with everything and everyone; and most of all, yourself.

You Are Not Alone

As a self-love starver, you have found it difficult to open your heart to others. You cannot find anyone with whom you can trust with your darkest secrets. Hence, you have been feeling all alone in this world. You believe that there is no one else who understands your suffering. In the throes of despair, you may even think that you are only one afflicted with pain.

On the other hand, it is also entirely possible that you have been dismissing self-love as a load of fluff. You would not want others to think of you as someone mushy and therefore uncool. Thus, you experience a sense of dismay at the thought of others laughing at you. It certainly would not do for the successful self-image that you have painstakingly built over the years. Grown adults do not usually confess to difficulties with loving themselves. So there is really no one whom you can talk to regarding your issues.

Lest you continue to believe that you are the loneliest person in the planet, please know that your perception is not quite true. There are far more people than you realize who are facing tremendous pain arising from constant self-beating, self-judgment and self-deprecation. You are not alone.

I have been receiving emails from people on a daily basis regarding their specific challenges with self-love for three years now. They have written in response to a post "How to Love Yourself in 17 ways" on my blog. What has been interesting to me is that self-love issues cut across all cultures, countries and ages. I have received emails from those as young as seventeen to those in their sixties.

The names of the senders have all been altered to protect their privacy. Nonetheless, the excerpts below are actual words written. They are as follows....

Evelyn,

I *so* appreciate the post. I googled "Love Myself" and your article came up first. Now, I know why. It is first class.

At 63 years of age, a minister for some 23 years on a full-time basis I still own self-dissatisfaction.

I listened last night to an audio interview on loving the self and it became apparent that love of self is the vital ingredient I'm missing.

I've written several articles on my personal blog that have garnered many favorable comments. While the articles came from the heart, I know there's a more fulfilling, zestful life that can be lived...but I'm not there yet.

Thank you for your insight,
Alan from United States

I am 28 years old, working as a Manager in a US MNC and earning decently well above average. I have been working hard to be where I am today. As compared to my friends and relatives, I am in an enviable position because of my career growth.

Despite the outward appearances of achievement and success, I feel horrible on the inside. I am so hesitant of any change, taking risks/chances and pushing myself to greater heights. I tend to give in to the demands from every friend and colleague. I suffer from a lack of confidence.

I am aware that I look up to those with better-looking features such as their height. I have a tendency to attach more value to their most trivial of achievements and undermine the best of my strengths.

At work, I know that I am able to do a job well, but whenever the situation calls for leadership, I feel as if I just can't live up to it. And so, I try to be a good team player but avoid taking the driver's seat at all costs.

I dislike the idea of being aggressive, rash, blunt, or boastful, but then again, I also do not want to be a person with low self-confidence, poor self-esteem and the biggest self-critic. Please tell me how I can convince myself that I am not as weak and undeserving as I now believe I am.

Warm Regards,
Pete from Spain

I am 18 years old and ever since my first boyfriend (he broke my heart), I can't seem to trust people the way I used to. It's really starting to interfere with my life.

I am now dating a new guy. It will be three years this April. He knows my situation and that I have trust issues but the fact that I have them bothers me. One day I'll wake up and love myself for who I am. I will trust him with every bone in my body. And then the next day I hate myself and I wonder if he loves me.

I have tried telling myself that I am a great person

and that I love myself but it NEVER works. Why is it so hard to love myself? I think maybe it's because I am afraid of loving myself too much. I really do want to love myself but I just can't do it. Could you help me out?

Yours truly,
Cassandra from Australia

I am a 31 year-old woman who has struggled since I was a teenager with anorexia, anxiety, and depression... I have never been able to have a long-term relationship with a man, and just realized in the past few months it is because I do not love myself...or even like myself for that matter.

After reading your article, I have made a vow to myself to really begin a quest to truly love and accept myself... Thank you so much! I look forward to reading more from you!

Sincere Gratitude,
Sharon from Sweden

I was crying all along because everything that was written there (in your blog), it was me. I do these nasty things to me every day. God, I'm still crying!!! You helped me a lot, extremely lot!

I'll just go to the mirror and say sorry for everything I did to me. Because I am good and I know that. I was searching help for starting to date or to make relationships at all, but everywhere they suggested that I should first love myself, dating comes just after loving myself.

So I stopped reading dating tips, I searched for self-love stuff instead and found yours. I'm sure my life's going to turn around, it has already by facing myself while reading each way. I don't know how to thank you for all you've done for me. I promise you, I'll be a better person from this very moment. Because I CAN.

17-year old Daphne from Hungary

Self-love issues show up in all kinds of situations such as in boy-girl, parent-child and romantic relationships, emotional and physical abuse, death, stress at work or in school and so on. These situations are triggers. When investigated into, the heart of the matter usually arises from one root cause: *insufficient self-love.*

You play out a life script based on your internal self-talk. Your words, actions and behavior are driven by what is going on inside your mind. It is possible to become trapped in the incessant stream of self-talk, so much so that you lose your sense of perspective from what-is. Your reactions are borne out of habit, more than anything else.

Indeed, I have come to realize that we live in a world starved of love. Not just with love for another, what is missing is also self-love. In fact, it is where all our problems start. Our lack from within gets manifested on the outside; and from our homes, to our offices, society, country and finally, the entire planet. Our internal conflicts multiply to create external environments that make us emotionally and physically sick. And it all starts from beating ourselves with a whip. We are nasty because we loathe ourselves.

A reader to my website pointed out that "self-love to be largely underrated but a prerequisite to being happy". I agree. Everyone has self-love issues, whether they are aware of it or not. Unless the person is a robot, there will be some conflict existing between the mind and the heart that has to be addressed. It is the thing that keeps us awake at night. It is the thing that causes us to overreact to a small trigger. It is the thing that leads us to being indecisive, confused and miserable.

Hence, if you identify with any or all the above, then please know that you are far from being alone. There are many people who also suffer from a lack of, or inadequate self-love. There are also many people in the world who are extremely unhappy. People leading lives where their souls are largely absent is a very common finding.

Signs of Low Self-Love

Self-love rests on a continuum. Since we all have some form of self-love issue in one way or another, the difference is a matter of degree. To help in your scoring, you may want to consider how you fare in the following indications of low self-love:

- You criticize yourself constantly.
- You believe that you are not good enough.
- You believe that you are unworthy.
- You find it hard to believe in yourself.
- You are excessively hard on yourself, but find it easy to be lenient towards others.
- You have got low expectations for yourself.
- You often put your own needs last.
- You feel de-energized, exhausted and ill constantly.
- When you look in the mirror, all you can notice are

your flaws, imperfections and faults.
- You cannot trust your own judgment.
- You are constantly worrying.
- You neglect self-care for instance, not caring about your eating habits, not putting up a neat appearance and so on.
- You have a negative attitude.
- You often operate out of a fear of rejection.
- You obsess over what others think of you.
- You cannot accept or believe in the compliments that you receive.
- You suffer from heart problems.
- You have anxiety or panic attacks.
- You cannot function well in social groups.
- You downplay your gifts, talents and abilities.
- You have low self-confidence.
- You feel lonely over long periods of time.
- You suffer from bouts of depression or sudden and inexplicable bouts of sorrow.
- You constantly crave the approval of others.
- You set aside your own desires in order to please others.
- You dull pain and feelings of unworthiness through addictive behavior such as smoking, sex and shopping.

If you have got more than three of the above signs or if any of the sign has an intensity level of more than 5 (with 10 being the most intense or true of you), you have some serious self-loving to do. All the talk about goal setting, how to be successful and making money quick is best set aside until you have sufficiently accessed the loving reservoir inside.

Life becomes more of a struggle. Invariably, you will face problems in relationships, health, success, career and wealth. It is hard to function well when you are your greatest enemy.

Mood swings, with a tendency towards depression, is a frequent occurrence.

There is a popular saying: *you must love yourself before you can love another.* You are likely to find the saying odd at first especially if it does not match with your experience. Indeed, your experience has shown that while you cannot love yourself, you have been able to love others. So the saying can be quite puzzling.

But, think of it this way. Love is compassion. It is a service. Obviously, it can be rather difficult to render service to others if you are in a leaking boat yourself. There would not be enough energy to go round, because you will eventually find yourself drained.

Alternatively, recall the time when you were sitting on a plane. You would have heard the following airline safety instructions over the plane's intercom upon its take-off....

In the unlikely event of a loss of cabin pressure or an emergency, oxygen masks will appear overhead. If you are seated next to a small child or someone needing assistance, secure your own mask first, before assisting others.

Well, I have a confession. I often dismiss the announcement as background noise. After all, there has been no change in message every time I board a plane. I would mentally switch off and read the inflight magazine instead. However, one of my friends, Galen Pearl, drew my attention to the announcement. She pointed out that it was valuable advice. I realized that she was right.

The instructions are extremely appropriate to demonstrate the importance of self-care. The announcement says to "secure your own mask first, before assisting others."

Perhaps the first time you hear it, it feels like an advice that goes against your gut. After all, if you are seated next to your child or someone who seems to be in a greater need, it is almost instinctual to place his or her safety needs first.

Yet, the instructions make sense. Prior to helping others to breathe, you must first be able to breathe. If you do otherwise, you limit your ability to truly assist others. It is hard to be of service to others when you are suffocating from the lack of oxygen yourself. In the context of self-love, it also means that the world does not stand to gain if you do not love yourself. The world only benefits when you do.

Self-love is food for your mind-body-soul, the nourishment that you need even before you attempt to do anything great or anything at all. It is a basic necessity. When you love yourself, it shows. You access the beauty, strength, grace and eternal nature that is you. By giving yourself the permission to be authentic, you also allow others to be who they really are. Through your being, you inspire others to love themselves.

Increasingly, a number of celebrities have been stepping out to endorse the message of self-love. They have realized its importance after going through some life challenges. By their stepping out, I am inclined to believe that it is because they have reached a deep well of reserves from within. And they are in a great position to share their love with millions of their adoring fans.

Take Oprah, for instance. She has interviewed a number on the topic of enlightened teachers on this subject. There is also the best-selling book, Eat Pray Love, by American author Elizabeth Gilbert. The book was turned into a movie starring popular actress, Julia Roberts. Finally, there is also the phenomenally successful Lady Gaga, who sings songs about self-acceptance. She shared about the practice of starting the day with 5 minutes of compassionate thoughts towards herself on The Ellen DeGeneres Show. The singing diva, Lady Gaga had the ultimate message, "Love yourself. Love who you are. It's all you've got."

My Self-Love journey

After I first made the serious commitment to love myself, I realized that I did not know how to proceed. The realization came as a surprise to me as I would have thought that I would be an expert on love and relationships by then. After all, as I recalled, I had spent much time in my younger days looking for the best spouse or romantic partner.

For a long while, I sought for love everywhere else other than from the inside. Brought up on a diet of fairy tales, I was seriously hoping to ride into the sunset with the One. I dreamed of being happily married ever after. Then again, my dreams did not quite materialize in the way I was expecting them to. I remembered failing miserably in my early relationships.

After growing out of puppy love, I went from relationship to relationship. The relationships would variably follow the same pattern. Swept off my feet by flowers, poetry and letters, I would fall head over heels. Soon, I started to believe that "This is It" and looked forward to sealing the relationship with an official commitment.

Well, after some months of dating, I would end up being dumped...ouch! The excuses given would often be, "Sorry, I am not ready for commitment", "You are just too good for me" and "We are not meant for each other" (can you believe that?). Dreams shattered, I would sink into misery. My world was crushed! Don't laugh, but I would spend nights playing sentimental love songs repeatedly, which stoked the raw feelings even more.

Spurned, I would spend hours plotting revenge which thankfully I did not carry out. I recalled receiving the well-meaning advice of "You should fight for what you want" from a girlfriend. That advice did not help much because I realized on hindsight that the last thing a guy wanted would be someone needy.

However, it would be the in-between relationship periods that I would find myself. I started learning how to nurture myself with self-care. It was also when I began my love affair with self-help books. Even as I found singlehood lonely, I realized that the periods of solitary afforded me a chance of renewal. I began to become more adept at picking up the pieces. I started spending my entire weekend taking up one adrenalin-pumping watersport after another and in the process, boosted my self-confidence.

After one too many breakups, I "saw" the pattern of my failed relationships. I was so afraid of being lonely that I spent most of my time hoping that someone else will give me adequate care and attention. Well, love received from the outside was never satisfying. Obviously, I had not known about needing to first build a healthy relationship with the self. All that outside search was made to fill the empty spaces inside my heart. I was afraid of being abandoned, and eventually, my fears materialized as expected.

I also realized the importance of revising my list of criteria when looking for Mr Right and I finally did just that.

Then, I met the man who is now my husband.

Well, the story did not quite end there.

Learning to Love Myself While In a Relationship

As I would later find – being in a committed relationship surfaced a lot more internal issues. Here was someone who was constantly next to me and with an incredible knack of "pressing my buttons". I realized soon that I was mostly fine on my own until and unless my husband started triggering my issues. Years of repressed anger accumulated ever since I was young erupted like a dormant volcano, which became active. When I searched deeper, I realized that they were issues about self-love.

What is ironical was that after being married, I began to wish to be single. At first, I was stuck in blaming anyone and anything outside myself. Blame soothed my ego for a while but I would later observe that all that blame did not make me any happier. From judging others, I would turn the attack inwards. It was traumatic. I became battered from the self-beating. The biggest casualty was my spirit.

Out of desperation, I decided to make a serious commitment to the self. My efforts in making personal changes did not amount in much previously. While the efforts helped, they could not sufficiently address my issues. It was time to do things with a lot more focus. That I did not love myself adequately was not an instant realization. I went round and round in circles for a long period. Eventually, I became aware about the cause of my problems on my own. The increased awareness helped me with greater self-love insights.

Fast forward till today. I have never felt better since. What has been interesting is that I found out that I married my soul mate with an agreement to help each other in our journeys on Earth. Through cultivating self-love, the relationship with my husband grew stronger. I also enjoy improved relationships with my children and everyone around me. I learned that a strong internal foundation leads to a strong external foundation. I now have the experience of love on the inside and outside.

It sounds cliché but my findings reveal the same findings. The discovery is that if we search deep inside our hearts for an honest answer, we will realize that we are all essentially wanting the same thing: *love*. However, many of us have been distracted into believing that it is things like money, looks, success or fame which is most important to happiness. It is possible to remain in this delusion for years. We choose to let love wait. In some cases, we even shut it out altogether.

Allow me to share the fable of the King with Four Wives with you.

Story: The King with Four Wives

Once upon a time there was a king with four wives.

The king loved the 4th wife the most. She looked the youngest out of the four wives. He enjoyed adorning her with fine jewelry and rich robes. He gave her nothing but the best. He spent the most time with her.

As for the 3rd wife, the king loved her because she was the most beautiful. He had worked so hard to win her hand as she had many suitors. The king enjoyed showing her off to his people. He brought her out for walks often. However, he always had the fear that one day she would leave him for another.

The king also loved his 2nd wife. She was his confidant and would often give him wise advice. She was also kind, considerate and patient. He also enjoyed helping her out whenever she had a problem too.

The king was a loyal partner to the 1st wife. The problem was that he did not love her very much. He hardly noticed presence. Still, he was not about to abandon her. He did not want his subjects to gossip or say nasty things about him behind his back. So he stayed married to her.

One day, the king fell ill and he knew that he was going to die. He thought of his luxurious life and wondered, "I have four wives with me now; but when I die, I'll be all alone. "

So he proceeded to ask his 4th wife, "Darling, I love you the most. I gave you the finest clothing and showered the most care over you. Now that I'm dying, will you follow me and keep me company?"

'No way!', replied the 4th wife, and she walked away without another word.

Her answer cut like a sharp knife right through his heart.

The sad king then asked the 3rd wife, "Sweetheart, I have loved you all my life. Now that I'm dying, will you follow me and keep me company?"

'No!', replied the 3rd wife. "Life has been good to me. When you die, I'm going to marry someone else!"

His heart sank like a ton of bricks. He felt sick in his stomach.

The king then asked his 2nd wife, "Dearest, I have always

turned to you for help and you've always been there for me. When I die, will you follow me and keep me company?"

"I'm sorry, I can't help you out this time!', replied the 2nd wife. "At the very most, I can only walk with you to your grave."

Her answer devastated the king, leaving him extremely depressed.

Then he heard a voice called out to him, "I'll go with you. I'll follow you no matter where you go."

The king looked up, and there was his 1st wife. She looked scrawny as she was suffering from malnutrition, care and neglect.

The king turned remorseful.

He cried, "I should have taken much better care of you when I had the chance!"

Now, what is this story trying to teach you?

Metaphorically, you have four partners in your lives.

Your 4th partner is your body. No matter how much time and effort you lavish in making it look good, it will leave you when you die.

Your 3rd partner is your possessions, status and wealth. When you die, you cannot bring them with you. They will all go to others.

Your 2nd partner is your family and friends. No matter how much they have been there for you, the furthest they can be with you is up to the grave.

Finally, there is your 1st partner. It is your own soul. It is often neglected in the pursuit of wealth, power and pleasures of the world.

The meaning of the story is as follows. Your soul is the only thing that has always been there all along. Yet, you starve yourself spiritually of love, care and support. Remember not to neglect your soul, for it is the only part of you that will always be with you wherever you go.

Towards Recovery

The period towards the first stages of recovery was not altogether smooth. There were many days when I felt really good about myself. Then, there were days when I felt like I have sunk into deep and dark abysses. The abysses were lonely alleys of self-doubt, blame, anger and resentment. I would get lost in the many corridors, with no way of knowing how to return to safety.

In deep despair, I would call out for help. And I waited. But no matter how long I waited, I was never lucky enough to hear voices from heaven with precise instructions on what to do. How unfair, I thought, that the supreme power would respond to Neale Donald Walsch (author to the best-selling book series, Conversations With God) and not me. The only sound that I could hear was the irritating non-stop self-berating voice.

One fine day, I decided to listen intently to my own internal self-talk. The voice inside my head had been saying a whole lot of things for a very long time but this time round, I paid more attention. I started taking down what I was saying.

Then, when I was calmer, I reviewed my recordings. I was horrified. While I already knew that I had not been saying nice things to myself, it was an eye-opener to see them in writing. Phrases like "I am such a failure", "What a loser I am", "I feel so useless" and "There is no hope left" filled my journal.

Luckily, I was able to muster enough courage to face my issues. Referring to these notes, I started working on myself. I applied the same steps – over and over again – whenever I sunk into misery. Amazingly, I began to experience energy shifts. The periods of inner peace began to hold out longer and longer. Soon, I found myself enjoying my own company. In a major turn of events, I began to long for periods of solitude. I have become my own best friend.

I have also come to know that my spiritual team did come to my aid several times. I now understand that energies of a different realm can work in unexpected mysterious ways. What has, however, been most clear to me is that I would not have awakened into self-love without having taken personal responsibility. Through asking for spiritual assistance and also working internally at the same time, I have strengthened my core.

The best part from having saved myself is the awareness that I own the resources to support myself. I am no longer on a Titanic, sinking from the lack of love. There is less need for struggle just to keep things afloat. What is wonderful is that I have survived episodes of self-hatred to now be able to share my story of courage, perseverance and authenticity.

And I would like to share what has helped me with you. Many of the descriptions in this book come from personal investigations into my own psyche as well as from external sources. Other than responding to emails, I have also helped friends, clients and family with the same awareness and tools.

The stories that self-love starvers tell themselves are typical. It is likely that they are the same ones for you as well. Even though your exact circumstances may differ, the thoughts are essentially toxic and the base emotions are essentially blame, shame, anger, resentment, denial, rejection and pain. It is a matter of intensity, no doubt. The level of pain that you are experiencing may differ from that of mine or that of others. However, you can still apply the same steps to shifting yourself into greater self-love.

Looking for Others to Fill the Gap For Us

Many self-love starvers hope that love from others could help fill their empty pockets of love. They want to be rescued by love. They want to throw themselves into the arms of another, who can address their fears for them. They wish for someone with the magic to make them feel whole. They want to believe that everything will be okay in a flash. Well, my opinion is that such wishes qualify as wistful thinking. In the real world, nothing happens until we decide to save ourselves.

I do not know if you are aware, that it can be a challenge letting love in where you are experiencing a lack of self-love. You hope to receive love from others but at the same time, your heart is closed to receiving. It is probably closed because of a past hurt or trauma. You are protective because you do not wish to be hurt again.

Love from others does not necessarily have to be in the form of romantic relationships. The most powerful love usually comes from the parents because it is less conditional than other forms. However, where parental love has been lacking, you are likely to long for a romantic partner who will fulfill your need for care. It always feels great if you can get someone else to validate your worthiness for you.

So we choose romantic partners who can help nourish us. In fact, we tend to choose those who can help nurse our childhood wounds. While it may not appear to be obvious, we invariably attract those who mirror our own internal issues. A deep investigation would reveal the same theme of insecurity, unworthiness and feelings of rejection separately in both parties. The relationship looks headed for disaster, when both parties do not warm up to taking both shared and individual responsibility.

When you are in a relationship, concealing secrets from your partner can get increasingly difficult over time. In a marriage, it is even worse. You are compelled to reveal the real you eventually. Living physically close to another person, you are led to exposing your vulnerability. It can be a nightmare. I certainly did not like the idea of someone getting to know how unworthy or insecure I felt. After getting married, I was increasingly taunted by my fears: What if he decides to leave? What if he rejects me after he sees the real me? What if he does not like what he finds?

I realized that I have got massive issues with self-rejection since young. It was no easy attempt - trying to repair the wounds of childhood while in a relationship. I almost wrecked my marriage. I would not recommend getting into serious commitment for anyone who suffers from a severe lack of self-love. Some prior healing work will pave the way for a smoother time when entering into any form of partnership.

What is involved in a marriage cannot be found in your

contract. It is not even stated in the fine print. Most certainly, your marriage agreement does not carry the clause that you are obliged to reenact and heal the wounds of yesteryears. It explains your initial lack of awareness. Hence, you only discover rather belatedly of the need to address your psychological childhood scars. It is the same for your spouse too. No surprises that a marriage can drive both parties to insanity when the wounds of each cut deep.

Unfortunately, there are no trial runs or practice shots. It is also possible for dirt to surface after a long period of being together. You are caught unawares because you fail to spot the signs. Eventually, when the shit hits the fan, you will be compelled to do what is necessary. You do so in order to save your marriage and if you intend to stop the cycle of being repeatedly abandoned, rejected and betrayed in all your relationships.

Self-love issues are often hidden. Projection is what happens when a loved one beams your inner issues onto the screen of awareness. You become aware that the safety of your inner world is being threatened. Indeed, it is possible to look strong on the exterior only to have yourself crumble by a disapproving remark by your partner. You are immediately transported back to the original childhood event when your parents said no to you. You tune into the same sense of rejection.

As it is, there would have been no faster way to surface all the deepest darkest secrets that you have kept locked. Your over-reactions offer you clues on which part of your childhood issue to look at. Being in a committed relationship will do just that for anyone. Marriage opens a can of worms. You learn most from the person or the people closest to you on what these worms are. You are challenged into revealing secrets that you prefer to bury. You are seen at your worst.

Living closely together, there are not many places that you can hide. Running off to a motel to stay for the night will not salvage the wreckage either.

Continued blame on your partner takes away the need for taking personal responsibility. Your egos become locked in cycles of conflict. Your partner's critical parent archetype puts you on the defensive. The more stressed you become, the greater your resistance. Thereafter, your psyche prompts you to build an impenetrable barricade around your heart. The ensuing conflict goes on and on with both of you defending your points, but without making any meaningful progress.

Most certainly, it would be nice to have your spouse or loved one make you feel worthy of love. You like being stroked, adored and hugged. You desire compassion for having suffered so badly since childhood. In support groups, one of the ways to help a person to recovery is to let him know that he is loved. The person feels good about himself, because of the support received from more than one person. The goal is to lead the person in pain to a space of self-love.

Well, what is key to know is that while external parties can fill the pockets of emptiness for you, you eventually need to learn to love yourself. You can never truly feel completely satisfied with the love from someone else. What is more is that you will strain your relationship if you are constantly feeling unworthy, miserable and angry. You become needy. You drive your partner away, if you do not allow him or her the space to breathe. Love becomes conditional when you are possessive.

While I was writing this book, I received an email from Nadia who shared her story...

I am single female who has a disastrous track record with men. I now recognize that I have been emotionally needy. I spend the whole time worrying about them leaving me. I tend to latch on the guys I date. When I am in a relationship, I cannot concentrate on anything else. I become obsessed and fantasized constantly about that person. It usually becomes so bad that I will scare the guy away.

I have no problem attracting men. However, because of my insecurity, I cannot hold on to a lasting relationship. I have got little hope. It seems that the right one is so far away. I cannot help but believe that I will never meet this person. Even if I do, I will probably ruin things anyway.

My last relationship just ended a few days ago. I feel as if I have now hit rock bottom. Obviously, being in turmoil has not helped me while I am at the work place. My career is also far from satisfactory. I am 40 years old with a life that is a big mess!

Nadia from Ireland

Ultimately, it does not matter whether you are single or already married. You need to learn to love yourself unconditionally. If you have previously suffered from trauma, find a way to open your heart once again. A heart that is filled with hurt cannot thrive well. To heal, you need to let love in. Love is a powerful force that renews, rejuvenates and revitalizes. It works miracles.

Eventually, you will get to the point where you are not merely in love with someone - love lives in and through you. The walls of boundaries that previously separate you from your inner self collapse. Being able to understand yourself deeply allows you to develop understanding for others too. Invariably, your relationships with others improve when you start to experience oneness with others.

The Benefits from Having Self-Love

It is definitely worth taking the trouble to learn how to love yourself. I cannot think of anything else more worthwhile spending time in. Studies have found that someone in love experience changes in levels of serotonin and dopamine, which are linked to feelings of happiness and wellness. While these studies did not make a distinction on which aspect of love, I believe that same results similarly applies to self-love too.

More specifically, the following benefits arise from having self-love:

1. Because you treasure who you are, you will want the best for yourself. This means that you do not withhold care that you need for yourself. In other words, you love and accept yourself completely and holistically. Consequently, you become much happier as a person. Because love is life-enhancing, your well-being increases, and everyone around you.

2. You are no longer stuck in the past. You practice forgiveness and compassion. Through releasing the past, you now choose to live in the present. Hence, you experience freedom. You are able to appreciate your blessings and enjoy your moments fully.

3. You enhance your ability to receive love. By knowing yourself as deserving, you are ready to accept love with an open heart. You recognize that your needs are as important

as anyone else's. There is a place for you in the world, after all. Receiving love from others contributes to your vitality.

4. You enhance your ability to love others. By being self-accepting, you also become more accepting of others. You become less judgmental of others because you realize that everyone is going through the same suffering. You acquire a deep understanding of the pain that others go through. As such, you are more ready to forgive others when they make a mistake. Your relationship with your spouse and loved ones improve tremendously.

5. You enhance your ability to become successful. Obviously, no one likes to go near a negative person. When you have a healthy and loving presence, others are naturally attracted to you. Your bosses want to promote you. Your customers want to do business with you. You strike more winning deals as business partners are drawn to your positive attitude.

6. You enhance your ability to reach maximum potential. Loving yourself leads you to realize the importance of honoring your dreams. Instead of putting yourself down, you are able to set aside your self-criticisms. By removing your greatest obstacle – which is really yourself – you pave the way to reaching your highest potential.

7. You discover purpose. It happens because you are in alignment with your true self. You own everything that is about you. You are able to express your creative potential meaningfully in the things you do. Because you now have a better understanding of your interconnectedness with others, you are able to use your gifts for the highest good of all. Purpose gives your life meaning. You start to experience an aliveness that you have never felt before.

The Paradox

After reading the benefits, you are ready to begin. Wait a minute - how do you get started? For one, you may find it difficult to grasp the concept of loving yourself. You face difficulty because conventionally when you talk about love, there are two entities involved. A relationship exists that binds two parties together. One party does the loving and the other party is the recipient of love. In the case of self-love, you ask: *who is doing the loving and who is being loved?*

Well, my book offers a plausible way of unraveling the mystery to the paradox. You probably also have a lot of other questions. You will find them answered in the chapters that follow. You will see how understanding the paradox, which is at the spiritual level, can lead you to deeper self-love. It is an inside job that also connects you with the divine.

Wherever you are right now in terms of self-love is fine. We can be sure that life will present the appropriate opportunities for you to evolve in consciousness. By being ready to open the heart to yourself, it is invariable that you will heal. Love is the all-natural ointment for your raw psychological wounds. Through healing, you feel good about yourself and soon, about everything around you.

There will come a point when you realize absolutely that unconditional love for yourself is the greatest love of all. Love is who you are. You have incarnated on Earth to know your true self by virtue of your life experiences. You are not aware of this, obviously, at least not from the beginning. However, you will eventually live into the secrets for transcendence. And when you do, you awaken into the miracle of existence.

Hopefully, this book will lead you to uncovering the most

powerful thing that you can do for the self. From reading this book, may you be guided to the answers that you need for an amazing life. As Hafiz, a Sufi poet who lived in the fourteenth century in Persia, once said, "I wish I could show you, when you are lonely or in darkness, the astonishing light of your own being."

CHAPTER TWO: GETTING STARTED ON SELF-LOVE

"Your task is not to seek for Love,
but merely to seek and find
all the barriers within yourself
that you have built against it."
- Rumi, thirteenth century Sufi poet

Dispelling Common Myths To Getting Started

If you have been trapped in a negative mental state for a long time, loving yourself is not something that comes quite so easily. Hence, self-love has to be a practice. To truly love the self involves a mind-body-spirit approach. This book covers all three aspects. This chapter is to help you get off the ground. It addresses resistances to getting started with loving yourself.

Your initial difficulties to getting started may arise from holding on to some myths. These myths are pretty common. The main ones include:

- As it is pretty much common sense, there is no need to learn about loving myself.
- Because it sounds self-indulgent, self-love puts me at risk of becoming a narcissist.
- Self-love means going for regular massage sessions to make me feel good about myself.
- Self-love is the same as having self-esteem.
- Loving others should be placed before loving ourselves.
- Self-love involves self-acceptance, which makes me no longer motivated to improve myself.

These myths have probably caused you to experience some internal conflict at one time or another. Thus, you are hoping to seek for some answers. The myths lead to the following questions. I have provided some clarification to these.

Question #1: Why don't I already know how to love myself?

Self-Love Secret: Do you find that self-love is a topic that has not been frequently discussed in your life? My guess is that no one has ever taught you the importance of self-love, nor share about how to love yourself ever since you were young. Try recalling the period when you were a child. Can you remember a time when your parents talked to you about the need to love yourself? It is likely that they have not emphasized the need for self-love.

You probably did not get to learn about self-love in school either. Year after year, you were taught subjects such as English, Mathematics and Science. You were also told that you needed to excel in these in order to succeed in life. Conversely, your teachers never got round to broaching on the subject of loving yourself. They cannot be blamed. Self-love is not a topic that is legislated as a requirement for core school syllabus.

All in all, you were given lessons on brushing teeth properly and made to give class presentations since the age of seven, but you have never learnt about self-love. It would seem as if the need to love yourself is implied. And maybe because it appears to be downright common sense, it does not need to be taught.

Hence, those with self love issues – likely, yourself - face tremendous challenges in knowing what to do in terms of self nurture. Now that you wish to get started, you have no idea who you can turn to. It seems that your parents would not be able to give good advice since they appear to be having the same issues themselves. In fact, it is probable that your ideas about self-love have been made through observations of their habits, behavior and actions. You have been affected by their inability to accept, much less love themselves in the first place.

Most certainly, lessons on self-love did not come in instruction manuals or how-to guides when you were a child. No doubt there is a ton of tutorials on how to improve self-confidence, do public speaking or set goals. You can find them in the bookstores, library or attend free talks on these. However, there are fewer valuable resources – if any – specifically on how to love the self.

My guess is also that no one likes to admit to having a problem with self-love. Most people do not like to admit having any issues, in fact. I would imagine that it would be pretty embarrassing to admit to not loving ourselves adequately to others. It would be tantamount to acknowledging that we do not know how to breathe or take care of ourselves.

Hence, while fundamental, self-love has perhaps been one of the fewer explored topics on this planet. The good news is that the spiritual consciousness of the planet has been rising rapidly in recent times. More and more people are beginning to be aware of how important it is to love themselves in a healthy manner. Perhaps the day will come when self-love is not only taught in school, but also sufficiently practiced by everyone alike.

Question #2: Is self-love unhealthy? Will it lead to narcissism and indulging in one's ego?

Self-Love Secret: In case you are mistaken, narcissism is not healthy self-love. There is a difference between healthy self-love and narcissism. The narcissist is someone who is excessively selfish with issues of personal inadequacy, power, and vanity. He is fueled on an empty tank. He needs to depend on others to make him feel worthy.

Conversely, someone with healthy self-love is not boastful, but who cultivates a sense of quiet confidence. If you love yourself truly, you do not have to depend on others for approval. The ocean of love that you draw on is pure, overflowing and eternal. You are in continuous touch with the essence of who you are. Self-love lays the ground for actualization of your full potential. You become much more able to love others and be of assistance to others.

You will also be finding out how the self-talk pattern of a narcissistic person looks like in a later chapter. If you have narcissistic tendencies, awareness is key in helping you shift into healthy self-love. In this book, the term "self-love" means "healthy self-love" unless otherwise specified.

Question #3: Is self-love simply about getting long baths, massages and manicures to make me happy?

Self-Love Secret: Do not make the mistake of believing that self-love is simply about soaking yourself for three hours in a hot tub filled with rose petals and with aromatherapy candles burning at the side. Sure, long baths, manicures, getting your hair done, and massages can make you feel good about yourself. You will feel relaxed and some of them are even necessary for you to feel well. However, these are just acts of self-care. They are external things that you do. The effects do not last because the fulfillment is only temporary.

Hence, it is possible to be engaged in years of self-care but still face difficulties with loving yourself. By keeping yourself occupied with spa sessions, you may even miss the whole point about what it truly means to love yourself. What you may well be doing is numbing the pain inside by continually indulging in your senses. You get an instant perk through these activities but they do not transform you from the inside. The rush of energy fizzles out rather quickly.

You move from one activity to another and having one

product after another. Even though each makes you happy for a while, you are never truly satisfied. No points to the many product advertisement messages that tell you otherwise. From awareness, you will discover that deep contentment does not come from the fulfillment of any material desires.

Question #4: Is self-love the same as self-esteem?

Self-Love Secret: I frequently see the terms "self-love" and "self-esteem" being used interchangeably. In my understanding, there is a difference between self-esteem and self-love.

When you have healthy self-esteem, your thought is "I am good enough" because you believe that you are innately worthy. Your thought originates from the mind. It is an appraisal of value. On the other hand, self-love connects you with your heart. From self-love, it is a deep knowing that "I am lovable. " A deep love for the self is without conditions. It does not depend on your relationship with the rest of the world.

Self-esteem relates to your third chakra, often called the solar plexus. It is about how you value yourself. It is about your personal ambitions, inner hopes and deepest desires. An internal struggle develops when there is a perceived conflict between what you truly want and what society values. You may find it necessary to give up on your own needs, in order to be appraised well by society. It is also possible that you find yourself excessively drawn to garnering a list of accomplishments and labels such as "doctor", "lawyer" or "professor". Thus, it goes to show that you do not have the knowing that you are intrinsically worthy.

The heart holds the seat of forth chakra energy. It is the middle of the seven chakras. It channels love, which powers up your energy system. Fourth chakra energy is about how you feel rather than how you think. It is the deep intuitive knowing of your innate lovability.

Low self-esteem is often related to low self-love. Root beliefs can be that "I am not good enough to be lovable" or "I am unlovable because I am not good enough". Hence, when dealing with difficulties with self-love, looking into issues of esteem is also needed. In my book, I try to cover both aspects.

Question #5: Why do people say that I need to love the self first before I can experience truly loving others?

Self-Love Secret: It can appear as if you need not have adequate self-love before you can love others. However, you would lack the capacity to experience love to its fullest possible extent. To awaken into whole-hearted loving, you need to first embody it. Giving has to come from a place of fullness. It is only when you feel full that you experience the spontaneity to give freely.

Giving is a reflection of your internal value. Each time you give, you are saying something about your ability to draw from the innate bounty of goodness that resides from within. And, loving your children shows your capacity to love fully and unconditionally. Hence, if you can love others, why not do the same for yourself? You must be able to give love to yourself from the divine well inside your heart.

While it is true that you still can love even with having little for the self, you will never truly know how deep a reserve you have until you go inside yourself. You will not get to intimately know the loving presence that you already are or be in touch with your soul. You will not realize how infinitely loving you can be. You will not be aware that your capacity for love extends beyond your children but for many more people – multiple times over. By not intending to discover who you truly are, you have essentially shortchanged yourself on the extraordinary experience that unconditional love can bring.

<u>Question #6: If self-love means accepting myself, does this mean that I would not be motivated to improve myself?</u>

Self-Love Secret: Far from it. When you truly love and accept the self, you would want the best for yourself. Let's take the instance where you are a parent. You accept your child and would want the very best for him or her. You hope that your child will take steps to grow in terms of learning and well-being. You also hope to teach the child about making responsible choices.

In a similar way, you will want the same things for yourself. When you have identified something personally that you are not good at, you would like to make positive adjustments or an improvement. However, if you are criticizing yourself, it is impossible to be encouraging at the same time. Hence, you will need to make a choice on whether you want to say something loving or something unkind to the self.

Which brings me to the next point.

You Are Unique

If you have difficulties loving yourself, you probably believe that there is little about you that can be lovable. You think that you are nothing "special", or as good as someone else. You have problems believing that you can be worthy of something better than what you are currently having.

At the core, you would like to know that your existence counts. You fear knowing that you are "a nobody". Being "a nobody" means that no one else cares. The thought makes you feel lonely. You desire connection. You abhor abandonment, rejection and betrayal. Your greatest fear is death, psychological death. It happens when you are being abandoned, rejected and betrayed. Life ceases to exist, at least in the mind. Thus, how good can life be if there is no more meaning?

A sense of identity is important to you. There is a desire to stand out from the rest. You need to know that you are more successful, good-looking, smarter or richer. This may not be obvious because your ego can act in covet ways. However, you will discover it to be true every time you make a comparison in relation to others. The act of comparing can make you feel more miserable about yourself, when you focus on your shortfall. Obviously, there can be no end to comparisons because you will eventually discover that there will always be someone who is better than you.

Your mind flitters from thought-to-thought of "not having this" and "not having that". The focus on "not having" makes it easy to overlook the details that make up who you are. Without a doubt, you have got many wonderful qualities. You already are a unique individual. If you think about it, there is no one else who has gone through the same life experiences, possess the talents you have, look the way you do, have the same exact shade of eyes and so on in the combination that you are.

Don't believe me? Well, sit in nature to realize this simple truth. No two leaves, flowers, hummingbirds, trees, river streams, swans, turtles or babies look exactly alike. Nothing in nature or even the cosmos looks exactly the same. Each living and non-living thing contributes an important part to the biodiversity of the universe. Yourself included.

What distinguishes you from the rest is that you have a mind. You have consciousness and you have the power to influence your reality in a huge way. You have the ability to craft a life that is based on your unique mix of qualities, values and gifts. It is up to you to decide what experiences you would like to have. You manifest by transforming your thoughts into the physical. Through focused attention, you direct the energy that brings your desires into reality.

There is no one else who is more intimately aware of your inner hopes, wishes and desires than yourself. Only you can know, without the shadow of a doubt. And you are the best person to take care of yourself, support your dreams and nurture yourself to your fullest potential. In short, you are the best person to love yourself.

Take Personal Responsibility

Self-love is personal responsibility. Thus, you cannot delegate the task out to others. You cannot ask others to do the inside work for you. A therapist can help facilitate the healing necessary but ultimately, self-love requires your participation. In other words, no one can replace you in making sure that you are well nourished from within. Self-love prompts you to tend to yourself, at the heart level.

To love yourself requires you to make a conscious commitment to self. You affirm that you matter. You affirm that you deserve love and that you are worthy. Without making such an intent, it is possible to remain stuck. You find yourself going in cycles of self-beating. On the other hand, a conscious intent guides you in an overall direction. You have decided that you are headed on a path that will lead you to a deeper space of love from within for yourself.

Taking personal responsibility means putting your conscious self in the driver's seat. This means no longer blaming others or delegating power to others over matters concerning your own. You take responsibility for the outcomes of your decisions. And when you observe the relationship between your inner and outer worlds, you will start to realize how powerful you are as a co-creator of reality. You become aware that you have the ability to chart the course of your future by directing your mental focus.

Make a Conscious Decision

You are worthy of love even though you have experienced shame, regret and guilt over some horrible life experiences. Memories of once having been crushed, traumatized, betrayed and rejected continue to haunt you. Understandably, closing your heart has been your way of keeping yourself safe from being hurt again.

There is nothing wrong with having kept yourself safe all this while. In fact, it goes to show that your coping mechanism is a healthy one. Yet, there will come a time when you need to open your heart. If you continue to keep it closed, you will be prevented from ever receiving the love that you deserve. You cannot have a closed heart if you intend to have healthy relationships with others.

Hence, make a conscious decision to open your heart. Making this intent alone is a spiritual one. It activates universal life force that works through your heart chakra energy center, which connects you with the divine. You will start to engage your heart, instead of only your mind. You will begin to realize that while knowledge can come from the linear mind, wisdom arises from the depths of your heart. Then again, it is not one or the other either. Decisions are best made at the intersection where heart meets mind.

Indeed, opening my heart to love has allowed me to experience the beauty and meaning that comes with healing. I would not have known how worthy I am, if I have not first made the decision to love myself. I have never been in a better state of wellness. Life has most certainly given me much more back in return, when I started loving myself.

If you have been closed to love, I invite you to consider what I have to say. Opening your heart does not mean that you become reckless, foolish and allow yourself to be bullied. Opening your heart allows love to flow through. Love heals you from the pain that you have been holding on to. The dissolving pain clears the space for more love to enter. Thus, by opening your heart, you give yourself the master key to be free.

CHAPTER THREE:
SELF-LOVE – BODY

"Beauty is not in the face;
beauty is a light in the heart."
- Kahlil Gibran (1883-1931)

Body Image Issues

To love yourself, you do not have to grow your bust line by three inches (if you are female) or be six-feet tall (if you are male). In fact, it has nothing to do with looking thin, perfect or gorgeous, or being able to fit into a pair of skinny jeans today. Self-love does not require you to have cover looks but it certainly involves feeling good from the inside. One thing is for sure. Should you have a negative body image, you are likely to starve yourself of love.

Body image is how you perceive the appearance of your body. What you perceive may be a different picture from what others see of you. It can be hard for you to alter your perception, if you cannot see what others are seeing. A positive body image leads to self-acceptance, self-confidence and self-love. A negative body image leads to self-rejection, self-criticism and self-hatred. It is hard to know yourself as something more if you are completely identified with the mental labels of "I am fat", "I am ugly" and "I am a freak".

Research reveals that as much as 1/4 of your self-esteem is the result of how positive or negative your body image is. Studies show that more females than males have body image issues. It has also been found that about 96% of women do not match up to the models and actresses presented in the media. Apparently, this has been the largest discrepancy ever existed between women and the cultural ideal. Thus, realize that only 4% of women genetically have the ideal body proportions.

Teenagers often struggle with self-esteem because this is the time when they hit puberty. Their bodies undergo tremendous changes and they are discovering more about their thoughts on the changes. They would like to know how others view them. They would like to know whether they are attractive to members of the opposite sex or not. If they have not had the benefit of finding a way to process the changes as a teenager, they are likely to carry body-image issues into adulthood.

There is nothing wrong with wanting to be loved. A desire for love is natural. However, problems arise if you over-identify yourself with a negative body image. Thus, you compare your body with others. You would like to know that you are attractive. You compare yourself to the people around you or even more unrealistically, with the celebrities that you see on magazines, television and movies.

It helps to know that many of the images presented in the media have been manipulated through the use of sophisticated photo editing software. More often than not, the picture of a typical female model has the breast enhanced while the waist is reduced. In addition, she is also made to look thin in parts that expose any fat. All in all, a model can be made to look gorgeous through airbrushing, enhancements, cut-and-paste and also, via the use of duct-tapes, and push-up bras during the photo shoot. The proportions are distorted to fit an ideal image of what a select group of fashion houses consider as beautiful.

Undoubtedly, you face an increased risk with developing an eating disorder in situations where you are constantly bombarded by marketing visuals on how the perfect body should look like. In trying to achieve the goal of attaining the perfect body shape, it is possible that you lose perspective. You become obsessed with exercising, dieting and losing weight and eventually develop a distorted view of body proportions.

Eating Disorders

Anorexia nervosa or anorexia is perhaps the most common eating disorder. It is more common than bulimia. Anorexia nervosa symptoms differ from that of bulimia. Bulimia is an eating disorder whereby you try to undo bingeing due to a fear in weight gain. A binge eating disorder is characterized primarily by periods of uncontrolled, impulsive, or continuous eating beyond the point of feeling comfortably full. While there is no purging, you are engaged in sporadic fasts or repetitive diets and feelings of shame or self-hatred after a binge.

With bulimia, you intentionally purge through vomiting, laxatives, enemas or other similar methods. The method of weight loss differs from that of anorexia. With anorexia, you want to achieve your ideal body proportion and weight through voluntary starvation, excessive exercise, diet pills and unbalanced diets.

Unfortunately, in your zealous quest to look good, all the unhealthy habits associated with eating disorders can create much damage to your body organs and systems. Damage can be done to your digestive system (in particular, your esophagus and stomach), your cardiovascular system (some functions of the heart), muscular tissues and your immune system. Anorexia nervosa deranges your hormonal levels, disturbs your electrolyte balance and generally prevents your body from getting the required amounts of vitamins and minerals.

Studies now show that almost half of today's teenagers and young men and women of ages 20-30 have experienced at least a mild form of anorexia. I certainly recall feeling awkward while going through body changes when I was young. Although anorexia nervosa afflicts more women, it has been found that increasing numbers of men are giving more importance to their looks. They tend to develop milder forms of anorexia; however.

Chronic self-love starvers are at risk of developing anorexia. If you constantly find your mind occupied with thoughts on your body shape and weight and if you find yourself displaying any of the above-mentioned warning descriptions, you may be suffering from some form of anorexia nervosa. If this is the case, do not hesitate to seek immediate professional assistance. In severe cases, anorexia can be life threatening.

You would think that famous celebrities, born with their good looks and their talents, would be spared. On the contrary, many of them confess to suffering from eating disorders. Some of them have even died from their disorders:

<u>Karen Carpenter.</u>   Karen Carpenter was an American musician, who was one of the all time great musical sensations of the 70s. She had a beautiful voice. I recalled listening to Karen Carpenter's songs when I was young.

Karen was "a chubby teenager" and genetically, she was not meant to be skinny. Sadly, for this singer, she only wanted a thin body. Her dieting began when Karen's doctor put her on a water diet, bringing her weight down from 140 lbs to 120, and further down to 80 lbs. She used to take dozens of thyroid pills a day, and throwing up the little food that she ate.

One day in Las Vegas, Karen collapsed on stage while singing "Top of the World". Everyone was taken by surprise. In the hospital, it was reported that Karen was 35 lbs underweight. Then only did Karen realize that she had a serious problem.

Despite making attempts to seek recovery, she could not save herself. Her body was already severely suffering from the lack of food, the over dosages of laxatives, the lack of sleep, and extreme anxiety. When she died, Karen was just 32 years old. She died of cardiac arrest due to anorexia.

Christy Henrich. Christy Henrich was a world-class artistic gymnast. She was once told by a judge that she had to lose weight in order to make the Olympic team. Desperate to move up the ranks in the highly competitive world of Olympic-level gymnastics, Henrich took the criticisms to heart. Her drive to lose a few pounds progressed to unhealthy eating habits and, eventually, became full-blown anorexia nervosa. Christy Henrich died of multiple organ failure, as a result of her eating disorder, at the age of 22.

Ana Carolina Reston. Ana Carolina Reston was a famous Brazilian model. She began her modeling career after winning a local beauty contest in her hometown in Sao Paulo, Brazil when she was 13. She was later represented by top modeling agencies such as Ford and Elite. At the time of her death, Reston weighed just 40kg (88lbs) at a height of 1.73m (5'8"). She had a body mass index of only 13.4, well below the index value of 16, which the World Health Organization considers to be point of starvation. At 21 years old, she had starved herself to death.

How to overcome Body Image Issues

Change Your Perceptions. Obviously, it is important to accept the way you look. While surgery can help improve body image, it does not take away the fundamental root cause of your issues – inadequate self-love or esteem. In other words, you may have gotten some surgery done but you can continue to feel poorly about yourself.

How you can help yourself is change the way you perceive about your body and yourself. While you may not have stunning looks that will qualify you in a beauty contest, you will be confident so long as you feel good about yourself. So embrace the parts that make you wince in the mirror. Find ways that will emphasize your strong points or more attractive features.

Assess Your Worth Appropriately. Refrain from judging your body harshly. Instead, appreciate who you are. Challenge the beauty images that you see. Realize that it is silly to assess your worth based on unrealistic body proportions in the pictures that you see in the media.

Shine from Your Core Essence. Understand that it is impossible to have the perfect body. Indeed, it is in the nature of the conditioned mind to always find fault with something. Know that beauty is more than surface appearance. What matters most is the shining essence that springs from a deep reservoir of self-acceptance.

Undertake Self-Care. Taking care of your own body helps you to feel good. Through proper nutrition and regular exercise, you gain a healthy glow. You will be attractive. Hence, check in on your body often and take appropriate self-care actions.

Above all, Love Yourself. It all boils down to loving yourself. Love yourself completely and unconditionally and you will not have to fight the idea of being the body that you are to live in. You are perfect the way you are.

Very importantly, address negative body image issues that you may have because it can lead to depression, social anxiety and destructive behaviors. When you obsess over how much you weigh on the scale or feeling miserable every time you look at yourself in the mirror, then allocate some time to resolving your thoughts and emotions.

Avoid waiting too long to address negative body image issues. Be alert to the signs. Admittedly, it is difficult to come to the self-awareness that you have developed an eating disorder. Hence, do not ignore the observations made by your loved ones about your dieting habits. Most eating disorders start out innocently. The sufferers begin with adopting a simple diet plan, which eventually become excessive. By the time they hit some realization, they would have caused much harm to their bodies.

Loving The Body

You are born with the body you have. There is no point rejecting it. There are things that you can change and there are things that you cannot change. And your body is not of those things that you can easily change, unless you spend tons of money on plastic surgery. Accept that you are not likely to wake up to being in a brand-new body either. Such a scenario only happens in movies and make-believe stories.

In one of my favorite TV sitcoms Drop Dead Diva, Jane Bingum (acted by Brooke Elliot) wakes up to a body that is plus-sized. Formerly in the body of a fashion model, she has to deal with looking less than perfect. In many of the episodes, Jane has to deal with loss in self-confidence because she can no longer be together with her former fiancé who happens to be tall and handsome. She has to learn acceptance of her new body and be happy with what she has.

You may opt for expensive plastic surgery but altering parts of your body will still not solve your self-love issues completely. Note also that striving for the perfect look can be addictive. There will always be body parts that you will want to change eventually, after your first operation. There are many celebrities who have gone for multiple nose jobs, for instance. Yet, they continue to suffer from immense issues in self-love.

On the other extreme, there is also compulsive over-eating. Compulsive over-eating is the excessive consumption of food, often thousands of calories at one time. In the case of compulsive eating, you have an addiction to food. You use food to hide your emotions, fill the void of emptiness and relieve your stress.

Not many of us tip over to a compulsive eating disorder but concerns about weight is a common issue nowadays. A friend of mine had to deal with obesity when he was a child. Stephen did not have a small body constitution, to begin with. He admitted to having a voracious appetite as a young boy. His friends at school called him names.

Luckily, Stephen met a few supportive friends when he became an adult. He started working out and watched over his diet. Even though he is no longer fat, the recollection of background laughter about his younger roly-poly self still haunts him today. Stephen's conscious attempts to will the self to think positively have not quite worked. While he looked confident on the outside, he was encountering massive energetic disruption internally.

When we worked through his issues, Stephen became aware that his problems on rejection have largely been unresolved. Subconsciously, he believed that he was not lovable. Growing up, he had never felt comfortable in his own skin. He would constantly be in self-sabotage because of the negative body image he had of himself during his childhood days. Consequently, he encountered massive difficulties with reaching a high level of success in his relationship and at work.

Smoking, drinking and taking drugs are other forms of addictive behavior that cripples you. They are likely to be symptoms of the root cause of insufficient self-love. Such addictive behaviors lead you to introducing poisons into your body. They are great at covering up pain. Thus, you use them as crutches to weather through stress. However, addictions are just temporary means that can provide some relief but do not necessarily help you to better solve problems or contribute to your wellness in the long run.

Loving yourself requires you to practice the best care possible for your own body. It means having a balanced diet and exercising regularly. It means trusting your body's innate wisdom. You trust the cues that come from your body, even though your mind tells you to overlook them. Trust happens when you observe the signals of your body in response to stress and thereafter take appropriate measures to bring about inner harmony and balance.

A healthy body lays the ground for healthy mind and spirit. You do not procrastinate to a later day for exercise or eating properly. If you ignore the needs of your body, it is possible to be so physically ill that it becomes more difficult to address your mental or spiritual needs. Basic sustenance, from which you can then thrive in all aspects of your life, is necessary.

By being true to who you really are, you will always be in style. When you at war with yourself, there is no way you can look beautiful. However, when you are at peace with yourself, you will be attractive. You gain a sense of inner confidence that also happens to be alluring. Hence, it becomes less important to follow the latest fashion trends or have the perfect body shape.

You are who you are, and you do not try to be someone you are not. In case you are not already aware, being confident is the greatest turn-on for members of the opposite sex. There is no need for crafty strategies to land a new relationship. You just need to be authentic. With great confidence, you are deeply aware that you are lovable and you are ready to receive love.

CHAPTER FOUR:
SELF-LOVE - MIND

"What a liberation to realize that the 'voice in my head' is not who I am. Who am I then? The one who sees that."
- Eckhart Tolle

Endless Chatter

If you are not already aware, you are constantly talking to yourself. Your mind is engaged in endless chatter. What you have been saying to yourself comes from an inner voice. You had been having internal conversations about yourself, others and your stories about the world. Your self-talk exists at the mental level, which affects you emotionally.

The inner voice constantly repeats the same script. A positive script reflects healthy self-love whereas a negative script reflects poor self-love.

A positive script looks like this:
I can *do* it.
I am worth it.
I may have fallen but I can pick myself up again.
I can succeed.
It's not the end of the world even if I have made a bad mistake or poor judgment.
I love myself dearly.

Conversely, a script that is negative looks like this:
It is just too difficult to succeed.
I am far too slow.
I feel worthless.
My life is worth nothing.
I cannot do things right.
I feel so helpless.

Most people have largely negative scripts. The scripts are made up of a lot of debilitating, self-defeating and limiting self-talk. Much of this negative self-talk is done subconsciously. Now, what goes on in your subconscious drives 90% of your actions and behavior.

Roman rhetorican and writer, Marcus Annaeus Senaca, said, "What you think about yourself is much more important than what others think of you". I find it to be true. If you think that you are worthy, you are more likely to attract positive outcomes. If you think that you are unworthy, you are more likely to attract negative outcomes. What you see in your mind is what you are going to manifest.

So Who's Been Directing Your Script?

The inner voices that have influenced your self-talk stories have been echoing since you were a child. Who do they belong to?

Your Parents and/or Guardians. You base your life scripts on your early messages. Your parents and/or guardians are probably the most influential people in your life.

The messages by them can be positive, such as notes of encouragement and motivation; or can be negative, telling you that you are no good or with little talents. If the messages have been negative, there are two ways that you can possibly react. One is to blame your parents and declare yourself as a victim for the rest of your life or the second, is to prove that you are good and worthy of their approval.

How you perceive and now react to life is pretty much directed by your childhood programming. Your programming influences your self-talk. Your caregivers had represented the world to you when you were young. And so you have been forming relationships based on what you have learned from your parents and all other caregivers.

Your parents, in turn, learn about theirs from their parents. Hence, you have accumulated layers of beliefs, patterns and behavior passed down from generation to generation. Even though these did not originate from you in the first place, you had essentially adopted the same patterns, behavior and attitudes.

Authoritative Figures. These are people that you look up to because they are older than you or who are your role models. One example of an authoritative figure is your class teacher. By now, you would have probably been taught by quite a number of teachers, since a big part of your early years is spent in school.

A teacher who constantly berated you for being slow could have caused you to really feel that way about yourself. On the other hand, a teacher who encouraged you even though you have failed in your exams, could have inspired you to make a shift into adopting empowering thoughts about yourself.

Friends. As a young and impressionable kid, it is easy to get affected by what your friends say. Your emotional vulnerability is also heightened if you already suffer from a poor self-esteem. The seeds of your negative self-talk may have been sown by the repeated taunts by a school bully or a slew of unkind remarks by a thoughtless friend.

The Media. If you have constantly been exposed to beauty ads on looking good and being popular since the age of 3, guess how your self esteem is going to be like if you do not have an external appearance to boast about? Not surprisingly, there are many depressed folks out there with problems like eating disorders, obesity and psychological issues.

Take Charge Of Your Own Script From Now

If you want your life to change for the better, then it is time to take charge of your own script. You can change the script that you have been telling yourself by choosing to rewrite your beliefs. Perhaps all this while, you have held the perspective that your beliefs are unchangeable since you find them to be true. They make up your reality. Thus, you feel outraged whenever someone dares challenge your story.

Beliefs are essentially made up of thoughts. When you habitually think of the same thoughts and when they become "real" in your mind, beliefs are formed. Beliefs can be positive and empowering or, negative and limiting. Positive beliefs can propel you to greater heights, while negative ones can send you spiraling downwards!

Beliefs are perceptual filters. They determine how you view the world. They also act as confirmations in your reality of the environment. However, problems arise when they are flawed, distorted or steeped in unhelpful ways. And most of the time, they are. Thus, you have a false representation than what is truly the case.

The mind receives information through your five senses. However, in order to cope and make sense of the massive amount of data coming in, various parts of the information becomes sorted, deleted and generalized. According to one estimate, incoming sensory information is reduced from 2,000,000 to 34 bits per second.

What is helpful to know is that your beliefs are not cast in stone. Your beliefs are made up of thoughts, which are essentially energy. In metaphysical terms, they are statements of desires to the Universe. As a human being, you originate thought in a creative process in your mind. So think of it this way: *If you can create thoughts, you can definitely change them.*

Perfectionism Issues

Your self-talk can also be influenced by perfectionism. If you have perfectionistic tendencies, you strive to be the top, error-free and produce work that is impeccable. You would invariably find that the standards you have set are unattainable.

Discontentment leads to suffering. The suffering is endless because you are never ever fully satisfied with your results. You are in the perpetual state of feeling incomplete and unfulfilled. Happiness becomes elusive, like some kind of unattainable dream.

Note that there is nothing wrong with wanting to produce your best work or hoping to present yourself in a good light. However, having a perfectionistic streak can have negative consequences. You are in the energy of "striving", in seeking to meet a certain standard; failing which, you would tear yourself apart. You strip yourself of self-love.

If you take a look around, you will realize that no one has been through life without having made mistakes. Making mistakes is a part of life. In fact, the more you make them, the more learning opportunities there can be. Yet, the thought of imperfection makes you feel unwhole, incomplete, discontented and ill.

Symptoms of Perfectionism

- You are highly critical of your own mistakes or if you fail to meet certain expectations.

- You cannot seem to roll out a finished product such as a book or complete a project because it is *"never good enough"*.

- You spend hours obsessing over some minor detail that no one else would notice.

- You have a tendency to focus on the 20% that has gone wrong and cannot give credit to the 80% that is going right.

- You believe that you would never be perfect in the way you look. You will never be caught in a photograph with your mouth open wide, in an embarrassing posture or having "crows' feet". Any picture of yourself with an unflattering blemish needs to be edited heavily via Photoshop before you can show it to others.

- You spend two hours editing three lines of words that never get published in the end.

- You downgrade your assessment of a product or service because you believe that your whole experience is compromised by a spelling error, a grammar mistake or an extra spacing.

- You are always finding fault in others.

- You believe that no one is good enough for you.

- You find it hard to praise or compliment others.

Works of Perfection

The fear of not being able to create great work stops you in your tracks from producing anything at all. You have an increased tendency to procrastinate. You often find it hard to make up your mind. Thus, you move from one idea to another, unable to decide which is the best. *You need to be, do or have the best.* The constant bombardment of magazines is not helping. You are made to believe that the perfect appearance means not having a wrinkle, mole or ounce of fat tissue. Consequently, you subject yourself to exacting standards that are hard to meet.

As a perfectionist, you have honed your craft to a fine art. You have an eye for detail. Each detail is important to you. Masterfully, you weave every detail into a tapestry with a meaning that only the few connoisseurs like yourself can truly appreciate. Invariably, you cannot help but turn your nose up at those who could not spot the difference between fine art and common fare. (Remember the story of the Princess and the Pea? The Princess cannot get to sleep because under the layers and layers of mattresses is a pea. Her ability to feel the impact of the tiny pea allows others to know that she is royalty.)

Indeed, as consumers, we value the work of the master craftsman. We pay for painstaking work. We would pay high prices for leather goods that take hours to double-stitch by hand. Or sophisticated equipment that has not only passed all lab tests in quality checks but is also sleek and ultra-cool in design. Not to mention, stunning clothes that drape our bodies fluidly no matter what awkward pose we strike.

Problems arise when you lose your sense of perspective, in your obsession for perfection. You leak energy from an inability to feel settled and find it hard to take risks and needed action. Should you tune in, it is possible to discover that the base emotion that you have been experiencing is shame. You project your shame onto others and become highly critical of others in the process. All in, you are in a restrictive, limiting and contracted – instead of expanded – state of being.

According to David R Hawkins in his book Power vs Force, shame is at the lowest level in the Map of Consciousness. He developed this map through kinesiology, after conducting hundreds (or thousands) of double-blind studies and mass demonstrations. Shame is akin to psychological death. It has the energy level of only 20. The highest is Enlightenment at the 1000 level.

> "The level of Shame is perilously proximate to death, which may be chosen out of Shame as conscious suicide or more subtly elected by failure to take steps to prolong life." – David Hawkins, Power vs Force

In shame, we would hang our heads. We experience a "loss in face". We ask ourselves, "How can we face anyone from now on?" And so we shrink away from society. We withdraw into our shells. Believing that darkness is where we belong, we choose to spend our remaining days there. Historically, from the earliest caveman days, banishment is synonymous with shame.

How to Overcome Perfectionism

Work on Your Thoughts and Beliefs. At the root of it all is the thought "I am not good enough". Chances are as a perfectionist, you have been contending with a little voice that says you, your appearance or work is never good enough.

There is nothing "wrong" with you. From a soul-perspective,

you are perfect as you-are, despite the human imperfections that you see. Thus, embrace everything about yourself – faults, warts and all. Bring awareness to your negative self-talk. Use energy releasing methods such as Emotional Freedom Technique for the releasing of negative emotions. A brief description of Emotional Freedom Technique is presented later in the chapter under Keys to Self-Love.

Look at the Big Picture. Take a few steps backwards to gain better perspective. Ask yourself if the detail that you are obsessing over is really that critical. Does it truly affect your overall assessment or experience of the product or service?

Changing your perspective allows you to know that it is up to you to perceive meaning. There can be perfection even within the folds of imperfection. Each pebble, starfish, tropical flower or palm tree may not look perfect in its shape or as if each is properly lined up in neat rows or patterns but together, they contribute to the picturesque scenery of a beach.

Set Reasonable Expectations. While you strive to do your best, refrain from being paralyzed by wanting perfection. In other words, be reasonable in your expectations. As U.S. philanthropist, George Fisher, said previously, "When you aim for perfection, you discover it's a moving target."

Understand that striving for perfectionism is not the same thing as aiming for excellence. Realize that you can be your own harshest critic. It happens when you do not allow yourself any room for error. Obviously, there is no need to exert undue pressure on the self. Bear in mind that no one is born superhuman. If everyone around you thinks that your work is wonderful as it is, consider taking these opinions seriously.

Thus, acknowledge your limitations. Also, avoid obsessing over factors that you cannot control. Setting excessively high standards adds unnecessary stress. A stress overload affects your well-being. Ultimately, the level of your performance reduces.

Learn to Laugh. Taking things less seriously can help. Learn to loosen up. Adopt a light-hearted approach to life. Consider this: So what even if you have not produced the perfect product, written the best article or grown a wrinkle or two? What is the worst that can happen? Will the world come to an end? Through balanced self-analysis, you might discover that you have been overly dramatic in predicting the worst.

Understand that You Are Work in Progress. You are on a learning journey, as everyone is. Acknowledge your desire to produce an excellent piece of work. However, never allow perfectionism to hold you back from producing, delivering or publishing your work. You can always go back to revise, make corrections or amendments after collecting initial feedback.

Learn to Get Past Yourself. So you believe that you have got an important self-image to protect. You need to look like you have got it all together. You are quick to label yourself a failure whenever you find evidence that supports your being imperfect.

Understand that beliefs about perfectionism spring from your ego. Your ego is not who you are. You are to learn about getting past your contrived stories, painted dramas and mistaken beliefs. And when you do, you would experience much freedom. You would have liberated yourself from untruths that have been stopping you from experiencing fullness in life.

"You see, when weaving a blanket, an Indian woman leaves a flaw in the weaving of that blanket to let the soul out."
– Martha Graham

Story: The Cracked Pot

A water bearer in India had two large pots, which he carried with the use of a pole across his neck. One of the pots had a crack in it, while the other was perfect. The cracked pot would only be half full while the perfect pot would always deliver a full portion of water at the end of the long walk from the stream to the master's house.

Gradually, the perfect pot became proud and could be heard boasting about its accomplishments. On the other hand, the poor cracked pot could not help but feel ashamed of its own imperfections. It was miserable that it was able to accomplish only half of what it had been made to do.

After two years of what it perceived to be a bitter failure, the cracked pot spoke to the water bearer one day by the stream, "I am ashamed of myself, and I want to apologize to you."

"Why?" asked the bearer "What are you ashamed of?"

"I have been able, for these past two years, to deliver only half my load because this crack in my side causes water to leak out all the way back to your master's house. Because of my flaws, you have to do all of this work and you don't get full value for your efforts," the pot said.

The water bearer realized that the cracked pot did not know about its own abilities. And so he suggested, "As we return to ter's house I want you to notice the beautiful flowers along the path."

As advised, when they went up the hill, the old cracked pot took notice of the wild flowers on the side of the path. It observed how the floral petals spread out in a smile, beckoned by the warm glow of the sun. It observed the bees flurrying in and out of the flowers. The cracked pot felt cheered at the lovely scenery.

However, at the end of the trail, the cracked pot began to feel guilty once again. It realized that as usual, it had leaked out half its load. Dismayed, it apologized to the bearer for its shoddy work.

To which, the bearer asked the cracked pot, "Did you notice that there were flowers only on your side of the path but not on the other pot's side?"

"That's because I have always known about your flaw, and I took advantage of it. I planted flower seeds on your side of the path, so every day while we walk back from the stream, you've been watering them."

The water bearer smiled, "For two years I have been able to pick beautiful flowers to decorate my master's table. Without you being just the way you are, he would not have this beauty to grace his home."

Many of us do not realize how beautiful we are even for all our imperfections. When we look at ourselves in the mirror, we can only see flaws. We would hurl torrents of criticisms against ourselves. In fact, in many instances, we judge ourselves more harshly than we judge others.

We do not realize that our imperfections are also about who

we are. It does not mean that we do nothing to improve ourselves, but what we need to realize is that our so-called "imperfections" also make us unique. We learn to acknowledge the beauty that resides in us.

CHAPTER FIVE: SELF-TALK PATTERNS - MIND

"Most of the shadows of this life are caused by standing in one's own sunshine."
~Ralph Waldo Emerson

Negative Self-Talk Patterns

Awareness is key. Begin by becoming aware about what you are or have been saying to the self. You will need to make a note of your own internal dialogue. Pay attention to your inner world of thoughts and feelings. If possible, write these down.

As you review your notes or go through the observing process, it is important that you avoid adding another round of criticism. You may be tempted to beat yourself once again. However, the last thing you want to do is to inflict more wounds. You do not want to direct more negative energy inwards. The idea behind creating awareness is to bring about change, healing and transformation.

Self-talk patterns that conjure fear-based emotions such as shame, sadness, anger, anxiety, and worry result in energy contraction, whereas self-talk patterns that conjure love-based emotions such as joy, peace, light and harmony result in energy expansion. Self-talk patterns that conjure fear-based emotions are said to be negative and self-talk patterns that conjure love-based emotions are said to be positive.

Negative self-talk patterns lead you to sabotage your own well-being and success. Should the talk rises in emotional intensity, you can be led to undertaking harmful behavior such as eating disorders, addictions and withdrawals from society. Thus, an unhealthy mind results in unhealthy behavior. Negative self-talk patterns can have the following emotional energy:

- Rejection
- Blame
- Deprecation
- Criticism

- Neglect
- Denial
- Pity
- Doubt
- Narcissism
- Annihilation

Negative Self-Talk Pattern #1: Rejection

I am nothing special.
There is nothing lovable about me.
I am such a freak. No one will ever like me. Least of all, myself.
I just hate myself.
I have no gifts.
I am not capable.
I am born unlucky.
I just cannot stand my own looks.
I feel alone and lonely, even in social settings.
It will be nice if someone can come along and rescue me.
I feel so separate from others.

Non self-acceptance puts you in rejection. You believe that you are fundamentally flawed. Painfully aware about not feeling whole, you are convinced that there is something inherently wrong with or missing in you. Self-rejection happens when you are unable to accept yourself fully and unconditionally. You feel unworthy, as a result.

Your mind is particularly focused on what is missing that you cannot shift into a state of appreciation over what you already have. You are unable to lay claim to your strengths, gifts and talents. Even if you are aware of them, you believe that they are nothing special. Thus, you cannot stand the sight of yourself in the mirror.

Spinning imaginative stories, it is possible to get trapped. You interpret every situation that does not go your way as a sign of rejection. Rather than check in with others, there is the tendency to immerse in the stories as if they are real. Consequently, you spend many hours in a shroud of depressive emotions; feeling hurt, misunderstood and unaccepted. Because you are feeling poorly, you prefer to withdraw from social groups.

Shame is a painful state of emotion arising from believing that you are fundamentally flawed and therefore not deserving of love. Your state of wellness declines when you repeatedly experience shame. Eventually, non-functionality becomes normal. You find it hard to keep up with a regular routine. Thus, you often give excuses for not being able to show up for group outings. Life has become too much of a pain.

Because you feel un-whole, you look to others to make up for the shortfall; only to be disappointed when they are unable to fulfill your expectations. Others are seen as having the qualities that you lack. You crave for social acceptance but at the same time, get caught in envy when you compare what you have to what others are having. So long as you perceive that there is a difference, you are convinced that life has been unfair to you.

It is the belief that you are fundamentally flawed that most trips you. As a child, it is likely that you are not seen for who you are. You were told that you were no good, "so ugly" that the hospital could have made a mistake by giving you to the wrong parents when you were born, of the "wrong" sex, "a failure" and so on. By the time you are an adult, you have accumulated a pile of labels that reinforce how valueless you are.

It could also be likely that you had received little physical demonstrations of love, forgiveness and acceptance, when you were a child. So even if there was no physical abuse, there could be psychological scars that had left you feeling abandoned, unwanted and useless. Things left unsaid could have also caused you to make conclusions about your undesirability.

Extreme rejection often leads to self-destructive behaviors. Suffering from deep despair, a person with extreme self-rejection issues can be driven to attempting suicide. The person experiences deep insignificance and hence, intense self-loathing. If you are feeling this way, please do not hesitate to seek appropriate help immediately.

One of my self-rejection issues starts from birth. I remembered being told, as a young child below the age of five, by my grandmother that it would have been better if I were born a male. She had expressed her disappointment not only to me but also openly. Her disappointment was that being a female, I would not be able to have my children carry the lineage of the family name. My grandmother would have very much preferred a male to be the first of her grandchildren.

My grandmother had a lot of beliefs that were inherited. While she had settled in Singapore, she was an immigrant from China and brought up on traditional values. For your understanding, Chinese culture places a great importance of the continuity of the family lineage. The family name is to be preserved through the procreation of males at each generational level. Back in those days, it was considered shameful not to have sons.

Don't get me wrong. My grandmother did love me. She was

my main caregiver, when my mother was out at work. She cooked lunch every day, even though I pretty much ate the same thing on a daily basis – plain porridge with fried fish – when I was a child. There was no outward display of affection but neither was I treated badly. I kept out of her way mostly. Her afternoons were filled with mahjong sessions with relatives and friends. My parents were far too busy at work, trying to make ends meet.

Nonetheless, if it were up to her, my grandmother would have preferred that my younger brother and I switch places. She would have much preferred that her eldest grandchild a male. It would later take me years to process how deep an impact her words had on my psyche. Subconsciously, I took the messages to mean that I was not very much wanted. Psychologically, my existential presence was precarious.

Of course, I have forgiven my grandmother who has already passed on. I doubt that I even blamed her at all, to begin with. I understand that she have not known any better. She was brought up on the same set of traditional values and beliefs herself. Back in those days and being a female, she probably suffered from discrimination and harshness too. Born into a well-to-do family, she did not inherit a cent from her own father either, simply because she was female.

Self-rejection appears to have contributed greatly to my eczema symptoms. Whenever I was stressed – which was pretty often - I would scratch myself on my legs till I bleed. I have had eczema ever since I was a child. While diet and other factors play a part, my findings indicate that my skin outbreaks are caused by the subconscious message of "repulsion towards the self".

Repressed anger in the form of irritation during my growing years also started to fester. Emotional irritation led to physical skin irritation, the experience of "skin crawling". I now realize that irritation over long periods of time can accumulate to overload any body system.

Naturally, I am not expecting any medical doctor to agree with me on the above analysis. I had deduced the psychological causes myself. One thing is for sure, though. Ever since I started treating myself using alternative means, my skin has seen better days. Relapses and outbreaks become less and less often.

Loving Yourself Through Self-Acceptance

> *"To be beautiful means to be yourself. You don't need to be accepted by others. You need to accept yourself."*
> *- Thich Nhat Hanh*

Perhaps, like many others, you have viewed self-rejection to be a good thing. You may have been using unhappiness with the self as motivation for personal growth. Any dissatisfaction with the self spurs you into working harder, searching for new solutions and venturing into something new.

Sure, this can work. It often does. However, this can mean that you operate from fear rather than love-based consciousness. Consider the analogy of beating the horse with a stick, trying to get it to move faster. Not wanting to lose out to anyone, you now run at breakneck speed. It is fear that drives you on the fast lane.

There is danger from using fear as a motivator. Taking the path of rejection for motivational reasons can backfire. You may find yourself in such severe self-loathing that you lack the capacity to shift into acceptance. It becomes difficult to love, nourish and embrace the self. You develop low self-esteem. The acceptance of self becomes contingent upon your "arrival" at a certain destination.

A better way to operate is from love. Love is a position of strength. You cannot be strong if you are rejecting yourself. You can only be strong when you accept yourself. By opening your heart space, you provide yourself the opportunity to be present your pain. You do so without judgment, labeling or criticizing. You develop resilience by allowing love to work through your fears.

Self-acceptance is being open to your experience as it-is. To accept yourself wholeheartedly begins with making the choice. You say the following courageously, "I choose to love and accept myself fully and unconditionally". Love as a healing force is activated instantly when you make the intent of self-acceptance. It weaves through your heart by repairing any brokenness, wounds or injuries and renews your spirit.

How to Practice Unconditional Self-Acceptance

Understand that True Self-Acceptance is a Sign of Strength. True self-acceptance is not a sign of weakness. Neither is it about condoning your mistakes. Acceptance is about embracing the self in a non-judgmental manner. It would be difficult for healing to take place if you are in resistance to yourself. It takes courage to accept yourself. As Ralph Waldo Emerson, a famous philosopher, once said "To be yourself in a world that is constantly trying to change you is the hardest thing of all".

It is absurd not to accept that we have weaknesses. We are human, after all. We cannot expect ourselves to be omnipotent. We do not therefore set ideal standards that are impossible to attain and beat ourselves up when we cannot meet them. We love ourselves enough not to inflict pain inwards.

As far as I know, all superheroes have their weaknesses. Superman's weakness is Kryptonite, Green Lantern the color yellow, Aquaman water and finally, Iron Man cannot do without his pacemaker and also has a drinking problem. Each has started out in some kind of self-rejection or denial. Yet each has demonstrated tremendous courage, will and perseverance in first accepting themselves. They come to understand that they have unique abilities and are essentially, not hopeless freaks. They have to learn to embrace their weaknesses before they can actually become great.

To have self-acceptance is to build an unshakeable foundation. Your presence is solid. You are rooted in your being. Even if others reject you, you are okay. You do not collapse easily. You have enough self-assurance to be unmoved. With self-acceptance as the roots, you stand tall and strong like an oak tree.

Accept Every Part of You. To feel better, you first need to accept yourself. So, ask which part of the self do you not accept. There can be parts or aspects that cause you to feel deformed, imperfect and ugly. The parts that you continually reject want to be loved. You are to learn to embrace, cherish and acknowledge by feeling-attention.

Self-acceptance is death for the ego. Through losing your illusory stories, you learn that there is nothing that you cannot accept about the self. Self-love is to be unconditional. It does not matter if you have an unsightly blemish, wart or mole. You accept yourself for who you are. You understand that being human comes with imperfections.

<u>Review the Past for Understanding.</u> For a start, examine the root causes of non self-acceptance. Through an internal investigation, you create awareness. You understand why you have been facing tremendous difficulties from the inside-out. You learn the keys to unconditional self-acceptance.

Hence, look into your childhood. Acceptance issues often arise from whether or not you had been unloved or unaccepted for any reason by someone you look up to. When you were young, especially below the age of seven, your caregivers mean the whole world to you. You rely on them for support. You are in need of approval, acceptance and affirmation. These are fundamental psychological needs of survival.

If acceptance is being withheld from you, it is very likely that you will grow up searching for it. You are likely to be always seeking ways to compensate for what is lacking. Your relationships with others can largely be influenced by your feelings of lack of self-acceptance. So you are hoping to receive them from your boss, friends, lover or spouse.

The sense of being rejected is not necessarily true. Your belief comes from the perception that you have been rejected. If you change the perception, your belief changes. It is up to you to accept yourself as you are. If you choose to believe that your presence counts, you will not experience rejection. Your belief is also that you will always be supported and embraced by life itself. At the heart, each situation that challenges your beliefs represents an opportunity for you to affirm that you accept yourself – no matter what.

Turn Self-Rejection to Self-Acceptance

Self-acceptance is foundational. It grounds. When you accept yourself, you are at peace with everything about you – your appearance, actions, beliefs, values and desires. You experience comfort in the space of your inner home. Self-acceptance is the sublime in-dwelling that allows you to be free to be yourself. You are free to explore your greatest discomforts and your greatest dreams, at the same time and without any limitations. Hence, self-acceptance opens the door to genuine authenticity.

It is only in the space of comfort that you can develop the capacity to love the self. Your value is not easily detracted by difficult life circumstances or instances where there is rejection. Experiencing worth, you pave the way to becoming your highest potential. From practicing the courage to accept yourself, you radiate.

True self-acceptance comes with deep insights. You grasp life's apparent paradox: the need for individuality as opposed to the need for unity. You also understand that individuality does not mean separateness and that you have longings both for an individual identity and for belonging to a group. Hence, you learn to co-exist both as an individual and as a member of a group harmoniously.

You do not sacrifice your own dream to gain social approval and at the same time, you pursue your dream with the purpose of serving others too. Ultimately, you are to realize that while you have a separate identity, you are one and the same in essence with everyone else. Your individual contribution counts. Your contribution adds to elevating all of humanity.

Negative Self-Talk Pattern #2: Blame

It is my fault for things turning out this way.
It is just my fault for making her angry.
Why was I ever born? I never do things right.
Why am I such a lousy mother? I cannot even teach my children well.
I have made so many mistakes!
I blame myself for causing the rape, trauma or abuse.

You have been conditioned to point blame. You feel justified to do so because it seems that everyone does it. Pointing fingers at others is easy. You want to be able to say whose fault it is. There is an object to target at. You want to be able to make people pay. And you want to be the first to point blame before being made the scapegoat.

But what happens if you make yourself the target of blame? With self-blame, you believe that you are responsible for things that have gone wrong. You charge yourself as guilty whether or not it is truly or completely your fault. It does not matter if there are factors beyond your control. Instead of pointing blame outwards, you berate yourself.

Understandably, it is hard to let go of the story on blame. It is like having an addiction. Repeatedly, you would reply what has happened in your mind. Despondently, you wish things have been different but it is not the case. You are unable to accept that whatever has happened has happened. Thus, you experience the need to crush yourself with the weight of the crime. As long as you perceive that you have broken some rule, you find it difficult to let go of the fact that you have committed a mistake or have done something not quite up to standard.

I have a girlfriend who has been stuck in blame for a long

time. She blames her family background, her husband and her colleagues for how her life has turned out. She also blames herself for the wretched situation that she is in. She finds it hard to manage her emotional swings. It would be nice to be able to share what I know or to help her, but because she does not wish to take ownership, it has been difficult to extend help to her. After five years of knowing her, her story is still the same. She has been draining herself empty by keeping her story of pain alive.

Self-blame makes you feel guilty. Unfortunately, guilt is a feeling that does not go away easily. It is driven by conscience. When you feel guilty, you dearly wish that the ground underneath your feet would open and swallow you up. Guilt is common among perfectionists. You feel bad when you have done something that is against your values. Guilt lets you know that you are out-of-alignment with your moral code.

There have been many periods in the past when I felt guilty for not being a "good enough" mother. I felt that I made a poor role model for my children because I have lost my patience, demonstrated anger and shouted threats. It was obvious that I could not deal well with stress. And so, I would cringe over the thought of being a less-than-perfect parent. This was a secret that I would rather hide.

However, I later realized that I needed to forgive myself. I had not known then what I am aware now. I had reacted out of confusion and ignorance, from not knowing how to better handle the situation I was in. And most certainly, I did not know any self-help tools to help myself back in those days. Blaming myself only made me feel worse. It certainly did not help me come up with better parenting solutions. What had helped me instead was learning how to deal with my stress, worry and frustration.

I have come to understand that there will always be things that I do not do well in. While I hold the intent to do the best I can when it comes to parenting, I choose not to inflict unnecessary blame or feel regret. In the meantime, my children have taught me so much about how to be happy. I am grateful to them for the wise lessons they have to teach.

Blame keeps us stuck in the past, old and the conditioned. It disempowers us. When we are in blame, we can lose a sense of perspective. We are basically saying that we cannot make a mistake, a poor decision or a wrong choice. However, as we all know, it is impossible not to go through life without having "failed". As long as we are human, there is every possibility of having acted unwisely or unconsciously. Viewed from a higher perspective, our negative experiences let us know that we are out-of-alignment. We are being alerted to know that adjustments are needed for positive shifts into greater happiness.

Loving Yourself Through Self-Forgiveness

> *"Blame is just a lazy person's way of making sense of chaos."*
> *- Doug Coupland*

When you are stuck in blame, you are unwilling to forgive. You cannot forgive yourself because you are living with the following rules:

- Not allowed to make a mistake.

- Must serve the needs of others before yours.

- You are bad or evil if you have not met up with expectations.

- It is wrong to forgive because it means condoning a mistake.

Take a moment to review the rules. You will realize that you will continue to inflict yourself with pain if you hold on to the rules. Forgiveness is not about letting yourself off the hook so that you can avoid taking responsibility. Forgiveness is about releasing the past in the now so that you can make a forward movement. Through letting go of the past, forgiveness creates the space for you to take responsible new actions.

In case you are not already aware, there can be many negative consequences if you choose to punish rather than practice forgiveness towards yourself. Because you deem yourself as having failed to meet up to standards, values or expectations, you are likely to build resentment with the self. Invariably, you have a tendency to subject yourself to endless scrutiny. It is hard to love yourself when you are enveloped in anger.

If you can blame yourself in the way you do, you are more likely to do the same to others. Should you call yourself names such as "failure", "hypocrite", "lousy", "stupid" or "hopeless", you are likely to say the same of others when they cannot measure up too. Your relationships suffer because you do not think well of others. Additionally, others do not like being near you because they fear being judged and sense your negative energy.

If you cannot be kind to yourself, you are likely to be unable to accept kindness from your loved ones. So there is the tendency to push others away. You find it hard to accept any gifts or compliments. You basically feel unworthy of love and affection. What you need to realize is an inability to receive can make it impossible for you to receive any blessings from

God or the Universe too.

Story: Release Judgment

The following is a short story by Anthony de Mello, a Jesuit priest, psychotherapist and an avid story-teller about releasing judgment.

"How shall I get the grace of never judging my neighbor?"

"Through prayer."

"Then why have I not found it yet?"

"Because you haven't prayed in the right place."

"Where is that?"

"In the heart of God."

"And how do I get there?"

"Understand that anyone who sins does not know what he is doing and deserves to be forgiven."

How to Practice Self-Forgiveness

<u>Be Willing to Practice Self-Forgiveness.</u> Practicing forgiveness sometimes can feel as if it requires superhuman abilities. You are just not ready to forgive, despite knowing about the wonderful benefits of what forgiveness can bring. It is not easy, I know. There have been moments or instances where I have found it hard to practice forgiveness, whether to the self or others. I was filled with self-righteous anger all

right.

The most important step is the willingness to forgive. Willingness is an act of grace. It opens the door to possibility. When you express the willingness to forgive, you are intending for an opening. You are allowing for love to enter. The opening is just wide enough to allow for a shift in perception, which leads to an energetic expansion.

You recognize the possibility that you may not be able to forgive completely or instantly. However, through willingness facilitated by grace, you give yourself the time and space to work out the differences that you feel on the inside. Over time and hopefully, you reach full understanding and unconditional forgiveness.

<u>Forgive in the Now.</u> As best-selling author Louis Hay says, "the point of power is always in the present moment". This means that you choose to heal in the now, even for things that have happened in the past. It is a fact that you cannot undo the past. What you can do, however, is to decide to forgive and release yourself from the past right now. You may have memories of the past traumatic incident but you choose to no longer let them affect you emotionally any longer.

<u>Let Go of Your Attachment.</u> Take into account that everyone makes mistakes. You are human, after all. Thus, you acknowledge that you have made a poor decision but have chosen not to punish yourself for it. You understand that past imprints are not you. They are simply scars left by the memories. Know that it is possible for psychological scars to heal. Hence, be willing to let go of your attachment to the thought that carries blame.

<u>Avoid Self-Judgment.</u> Making a mistake does not mean that

you are a bad, evil or lousy person. Consider making the distinction between who you are and from the things you do. It simply means that you are not your "crime". In other words, you are not defined by having made a poor choice or decision.

Turn Self-Blame to Self-Forgiveness

Most certainly, it does not help to dwell in guilt, which self-blame carries on its back. Excessive guilt can paralyze you into inaction. Stricken with guilt, you have not been able to take any positive action thereafter. You also become fearful of making new mistakes. You are unwilling to take risks. Hence, you rob yourself of living life as an adventure.

Consider creating a ritual or ceremony to demonstrate the act of forgiveness. It seals the energy of the old and puts you on a new start. One ritual that you can do is to list down all the things that you would like to forgive yourself on a piece of paper. Then, burn the piece of paper as a symbolic act of intent.

Self-blame is toxic for your heart. Forgiveness is important for your inner health. If you have indeed made some mistakes in the past, healing can be made through forgiveness. You have to forgive wholeheartedly. Self-forgiveness is kindness that you give inwards. It is the healing balm you apply when you perceive that you have fallen short. You not only forgive yourself but all others who have contributed to the situation that you are now in.

Self-forgiveness is an act of grace by your soul. By inviting grace, your soul is being generous with itself. Where there is generosity, there is no more lack. You are not deficient in love. It just takes a crack in the door for grace to enter. Soon, love overflows. There is a warm rush of comfort. No longer in torture, you are at peace with yourself.

Negative Self-Talk Pattern #3: Deprecation

I look down on myself.
I am worth peanuts.
I feel ashamed about myself.
I am never good enough.
No matter what I do, I can never be up to scratch.
If there is one thing that I am ever right is this: I am a failure.

Self-deprecation leads you to putting yourself down. You view the self in the most unflattering light. Self-deprecation carries the energy of disdain, scorn and contempt. Targeted inwards, your words bring your spirit down. Many comedians are known to use self-deprecating humor deliberately in order to bridge a connection with the audience.

However, repeatedly belittling yourself is a sure sign of inferiority complex. You have low self-esteem. You genuinely believe in the disparaging remarks that you have been making about yourself. You feel as if you are a complete and utter failure. Experiencing a lack of confidence, you have little belief in your abilities. And you truly think that you are worth less than others.

If you grow up being criticized, had lack of approval and not given attention, you are likely to end up with major self-deprecation issues. The negative childhood message that you received often is that you are not "good enough". Your parents and caregivers are likely to be perfectionists or want you to be perfect. They are likely to suffer from low esteem too. Thus, you were often plagued with embarrassment and shame over your frequent "failures" or your inability to meet expectations.

You have hoped to please your parents. You learned to obtain nods of approval through achievement and performance. In the end, you decided that it did not matter what your dreams were. Rather, it was more important to pursue a career just to make your parents proud. Yet no matter how much you do thereafter, it still appears as if they are never good enough for your parents.

From a young age, you have learned to recognize what the activities that would win you extra points were. And so you expend much of your energy on these. It was important for you to be liked and accepted socially. Over time, you became terrified of letting others see the real you. You prefer that others know you as someone who is confident, together and self-assured, not as someone who is extremely insecure, confused and imperfect.

Having an inferiority complex can cause you a lot of issues in social settings. You have problems developing healthy relationships. You find it hard to make new friends and with old friends, you face tremendous difficulty with expressing your needs. Self-deprecation can also cause you to constantly apologize about yourself to others. In this case, your front of humility is just a cover-up to hide your deep sense of insecurity.

Invariably, the constant comparing against others eats at you. You strive to prove your worth, but it is a futile exercise. No matter how many qualifications you acquire, how rich you become or how many accolades you receive, it is still possible to feel as if you can never match up. So long as you continue to suffer from low self-esteem, an external search for validation can never make you feel whole.

Because you believe that you are lacking, it is possible that you look up to others in areas that you fall short in. Self-deprecation is likely to lead you to overestimating the worth of others. In your relationships, you feel as if you are in a subservient position and seldom on equal footing. And so, you idolize others with blind adulation. However, blind adulation causes you to give your power away. It also constitutes energy leakage. Your hero-worship of others masks the low self-esteem you suffer from.

Self-deprecation causes you to have a poor attitude towards life. You fear new adventures. You freeze if you have to encounter anything outside your comfort zone. You worry excessively over the possibility of a loss of face. Sensitive to criticisms, you take what others to say to heart. Thus, the slightest negative remark by others about you is viewed as an attack. You crumble easily.

The Image of Success

Perhaps all along, you have found it important to cultivate the image of success. Success can mean different things to different people. For many of us, success means having a big house, a nice car and lots of money. For others, it may mean academic qualifications. Whatever it means, you believe that it is crucial that you convey the meaning most significant to you in a public persona.

Serena came from a poor background. She used to lament over not having the chance to go to University. Even though she married into a well-to-do family, she continued to suffer from low self-esteem. Serena never quite felt that she belonged, though. During extended family dinners, she faked her interest in the heavy topics discussed. She also forced herself to laugh at the jokes cracked and pretended that she had read some of the books that others on the table talked about.

In a bid to boost her worthiness, Serena went on shopping sprees. She felt that it was important to be part of the new social circle that she was in. Serena got to know several of the wives of her husband's business associates. And so she needed the branded bags, designer clothes and expensive shoes to look the part.

Serena was also introduced to plastic surgery. She noticed that the Botox injections helped to erase some of her fine lines. Even though she needed regular maintenance, she was rather pleased with the results. Serena noted with satisfaction that the lines were no longer showing up in photo close-ups.

As luck would have it, her fortune turned. The financial crisis bankrupted her family's business. Her husband had to close down his company. He was also forced to sell the investment properties they once held. From living in a bungalow, they took the painful decision of downsizing to a small apartment. Understandably, she had many arguments with her husband.

Picking up the pieces was hard. From having everything that money could afford, she now had very little. Her rich girlfriends stopped calling her, ever since they found out her situation. Serena might have felt the hollowness inside for years but she had never ever sought help. This time, she knew that she could not procrastinate anymore. Her self-esteem had sunk to an all-time historic low.

Like Serena, can the fear of being considered "a nobody" be haunting you too? You are intensely afraid of having little or no worth. So it is important that you look as if you have it all together. You want to be seen as successful or attractive. You want to be assured that you are valued, approved and accepted. You desire huge public support in the things that you do.

Any sign of vulnerability is seen as a weakness. Few people enjoy the prospect of appearing vulnerable. And you are no different. However, without owning up to your vulnerabilities, it is hard to accept yourself as you are. And so you hide your true self behind false pretenses. Not to win in a game constitutes a loss in face. The more successful the self-image is, the greater the dependency on it that you are likely to develop for a sense of worthiness. Consequently, losing a game conjures shame and triggers feelings of low worthiness.

To release all false concepts of the self is to be authentic. Authenticity involves embracing yourself as you really are. You are true to yourself and no longer fear rejection. You no longer give excuses nor express shame for being "different". It is okay to be vulnerable. It is okay for others to know about your imperfections too. You value the fact that you are unique. You believe that you are deserving of unconditional love because you are worthy.

Loving Yourself Through Self Esteem

> *"Yours is the energy that makes your world. There are no limitations to the self except those you believe in."*
> *- Jane Roberts*

Self-esteem is about appraising yourself in relation to others. Your beliefs about the self arise from thought. Hence, to raise your self-esteem, what you can do is to examine your thoughts. By altering your thoughts, you can possibly change your perception about the self.

Self-esteem is the value you place on the self as a worthy person. Low self-esteem can affect every part of your life. Like many others, you have found yourself to be much happier with a high self-esteem. You determine your worth by the grades you get in an exam, how successful you are in your career, the amount of money you make and whether or not you have lots of friends.

More often than not, how you are doing is used to determine how you feel about the self. You depend on external indicators of success to decide on how you rate the self. Low self-worth reduces your capacity to enjoy life. On a good day, when you receive heaps of praise, you feel good about yourself and your self-esteem skyrockets. However, when you receive a negative comment, you feel bad and your world comes crashing down. It does not matter if it is just a single feedback out of a ton of positive ones that you got during the day.

While your emotions may fluctuate day-to-day, your self-esteem does not. Those with low self-esteem need external validation to determine how good they feel about themselves. They will soon realize that the positive emotions do not last. Material possessions or status can never fill the void that you face inside from deeming yourself as unworthy.

Having healthy self-esteem is being able to perceive your worth, regardless of conditions. It can make a tremendous difference to the quality of your life when you have healthy self-esteem. When you have healthy self-esteem, you have high regard for yourself as well as others. You treat everyone equally and fairly, regardless of how successful or wealthy they are.

Your psychological survival depends on the whether you have an edge over others. Your ego constantly craves a diet of external validation, attention and gratification. When you have an exaggerated sense of self-importance, you swell with pride. Self-esteem in this case is not healthy.

Self-esteem is more than just confidence. Confidence is a product of having high self-esteem. If you have healthy self-esteem, you are likely to be more confident. However, if you are confident, it does not necessarily mean that you have high self-esteem. It is possible that you portray a picture of confidence to the public but internally, you feel terrible about yourself.

Hence, you can be confident in solving complex Mathematic equations but you may still have a self-esteem issue. You can be confident playing a lead role but you can feel desperately insecure off-stage. In a similar way, models can appear to exude confidence on the catwalk but privately, suffer from anorexia nervosa springing from a case of low self-esteem. Hence, the receipt of public attention is no guarantee of self-love and esteem.

Self-esteem is having the strength in confidence that you have the ability to handle anything that life throws at you. You do not go weak in the knees at the sound of trouble. And even if you encounter setbacks, you have the ability to pick yourself up fairly quickly. You are resilient because you have a high sense of self-worth.

How to build Self-Esteem

Before you run yourself down again, consider stopping for a moment. Assess the negative impact that a low self-esteem has on the quality of your life so far. Make the decision to address your worthiness issues:

Examine Your Beliefs. When you have healthy self-esteem, you believe that you are worthy and are able to accept yourself unconditionally. Essentially, your belief is that "I am good enough". You value yourself irrespective of conditions. How you feel and believe about the self determines your outcomes. If you believe that you are loved and are lovable, you are more likely to be supported by life. Because you feel deserving, you are more likely to ask for help when needed. Believing in yourself, you are better able to accomplish goals and perform better in schools and later on, at work.

Challenge Your Assumptions. Let your achievements speak for themselves. Also be aware about the expectations that you have set for the self. Are they realistic? Are they humanly possible to achieve?

Acknowledge Your Strengths, Talents and Achievements. Take the time to list down your accomplishments. It can be easy brushing your accomplishments aside. You find it hard to give yourself credit. One great idea is to ask a bunch of supportive friends to tell you what your strengths are.

Visualize Success. Picture yourself as someone successful and with healthy self-esteem. It is better to focus your energy on a positive picture rather than on how bad you feel about yourself. The better you are in redirecting your thoughts, the greater your ability to turn your mental picture of success into reality.

Turn Self Deprecation to Self Esteem

Advertising media will often impress on you that the more you accumulate, the more worthy you become. And so you are told that you need more designer handbags, expensive face creams and an impressive collection of shoes. You are told that you need these items in order to attract a member of the opposite sex, win a sale or impress your boss. Well, should you believe in these messages, you are going to be sorely disappointed.

To be free is to be able to release the belief that your value is dependent on the validation of others. You become inner-directed rather than rely on external props. It is possible to experience a hollow feeling at first. However, as you stay with this process, you will be able to dismantle the pain beneath the false appearance of success.

Your foundation is strong when you have healthy self-esteem. External factors do not derail or threaten you easily. You are able to assess your position based on an honest assessment of your abilities and limitations. No longer feeling the need to live up to the expectations of others, you experience freedom. The love that you receive from others feels more real because it is the authentic self that others come into contact with.

From a spiritual perspective, low self worth happens when you have no awareness of your divine self. Ultimately, you are to know that you are no different from anyone else. The same life force flows through you. Hence, worth is something that you already are. Just like any other person, you have the ability to tap into the same energy. You have the ability to harness the flow in alignment with your higher purpose in life. Hence, you step back into power upon ownership of your divinity.

It is possible to be physically wealthy but spiritually poor. Your true worth comes from the inside. The true measure of worth is the divinity in you – which is infinite. In fact, it is why you have incarnated. Your spiritual journey on Earth is to recall who you are. Through self-awareness, you are in touch with your intrinsic nature. By virtue of your life experiences, you awaken into the true worth of your essence.

Negative Self-Talk Pattern #4: Criticism

I am way too stupid.
I am a slow learner.
I just cannot do it.
What was I thinking? I will never be accepted for who I am.
It's not as if I have stellar looks. Who would take notice of me?
What made me say that? I hate myself for looking like a fool.
I am too fat.
I am too thin.
I cannot believe I did that. I hate making mistakes.
I have to be perfect.
I must obey this rule.

It is estimated that an average person makes between 300 to 400 self-evaluations per day. Unfortunately, for most of us, the evaluations have been largely unkind. Research suggests that for the average person 80% of self-evaluations are negative, with only 20 percent as positive. Hence, it can be deduced that you have largely been dissatisfied with who you are.

With chronic self-criticism, you have a debilitating tendency to put yourself down. You attack the self with harsh words. You invariably inflict pain, guilt and fear. At the extreme, you are contemptuous of the self. Your inner talk is like venom, eroding any love energy that you can otherwise embrace yourself with. You are the judge and the person on trial - rolled into one. As if you are in some kind of criminal proceedings, you have an innate ability to shred the self to pieces.

Where you have got perfectionism issues, you are more likely to subject yourself to intense scrutiny. You can tell if this is true of yourself if you often find yourself experiencing righteous anger. And so you are able to know if you have been applying a strict set of rules, expectations and standards. Internally, you draw up long list of criteria on what is acceptable and what is not. There is a "right" and there is a "wrong". You are ruled by "shoulds" and "musts".

If you are prone to criticizing yourself, you are probably having body image issues too. You cannot help but perceive that you are less than whole because of some body part that is seemingly imperfect. The "imperfection" may not necessarily be true. What counts is your perception. Your perception determines what you say to the self. You are not able to look at your own reflection in the mirror without some criticisms about your appearance.

Undoubtedly, you are better at making yourself feel worse than better. Your mind has a tendency to focus on the one thing that you have done poorly, ignoring the majority of the positive things that you have done well. You tend to discount your successes. Should you receive praise, your tendency is to brush your accomplishments aside with "Oh, it was nothing", "I was just plain lucky" and "Anyone could have done better than me".

You are angry with yourself for not being able to conform to the ideals. Your self-talk pattern reflects the anger, irritation and frustration you have with the self, when you violate your own rules or fail to meet your standards. There is possibly a part of your self that is not keen on personal development. Yet, failing to make continuous improvement drives you to experience extreme guilt and shame.

Loving Yourself Through Self-Compassion

> *"Criticism, like rain, should be gentle enough to nourish a man's growth without destroying his roots."*
> *- Frank Howard Clark*

Having self-compassion is not something that you are used to. After all, you have been in the habit of beating yourself up all your life. In your experience, you have found harsh criticisms extremely useful as a motivator for actions. It is how you have made yourself get out of bed every morning. However, if you have been criticizing yourself and your life continues to suck, try approving yourself for a change.

You may perceive self-compassion as being indulgent. You would not dream of giving excuses for your wretched state. You see self-compassion as disempowering. You do not like the idea of being a softie. Hence, you have found it necessary to take a tough stance towards the self.

Then again, you may not be aware that recent studies show that those who are self-compassionate are more productive, have lower stress levels and produce 100% more anti-aging hormones. Apparently, feeling compassionate controls inflammatory responses in the body, postulated by most scientists to be connected with many serious diseases, especially cardiovascular diseases.

In addition, contrary to widespread belief, those who are self-compassionate are more motivated to persevere. Self-compassionate people may even be open access to higher levels of creative thinking, suggests one study in the Creativity Research Journal. Hence, I do not see any logical reasons why anyone should not practice more compassion.

What is Compassion

Let us examine what compassion is. I liken compassion to be a generous outpouring of the soul's unconditional love for healing in the face of suffering. In a state of empathy, you have the ability to see and feel the pain of others, as if it is your own. You experience deep concern. When you are compassionate, you are filled with rawness, connection and tenderness. You also have the awareness of contrast and a sense of shared human connection.

Extending love and kindness does not necessarily mean bestowing another person with gifts but it is the show of gentleness and the generosity of the spirit. An easy way to bring up the feeling of compassion is to recall the time when you first heard the news of a tsunami, earthquake or some other natural disaster. Upon hearing the news, you cannot help but experience an emotional tear in your heart, and you feel called to assist immediately.

You experience compassion when you realize that someone else is in worse trouble than you. It leads you to becoming aware of the contrast in both your circumstances. The moment of awareness puts you in touch with the realities of life: ups and downs, joys and sorrows, and also, dreams and crushed hopes. By seeing how bad a situation can turn for someone else, you develop a sense of appreciation for the blessings that you currently enjoy. You learn not to take what you have for granted.

In the face of adversity, you realize how powerless you can be. You recognize that there sometimes can be unexplainable factors that are beyond anyone's control. Your heart becomes open to the raw feelings of vulnerability, an experience available by virtue of being human. You feel for the person in suffering, no matter how near or far he or she is.

With compassion, you become in touch with what is real. There is deep empathy for the suffering that goes on behind the scenes. You are able to touch the core inside yourself that hopes for the best for others. You are able to connect with the desires in others, the same things that you want for yourself too. Inadvertently, you unite in the feeling of oneness.

What Is Self-Compassion

To let go of criticism, you need to be aware of your inner dialogue. Admittedly, it is not easy giving the self an honest evaluation without tipping over to criticism. Most of us either conveniently overlook our own faults or become excessively harsh on ourselves. What is to know is that a balance needs to be maintained. A growing body of research suggests the self-compassion, rather than criticism, leads to better outcomes in the long run.

Self-compassion allows you to be nourished quietly from the inside. You become gentle with yourself. You accept and care deeply for the self. Self-compassion allows you to see that like every one else, you are just as imperfect. Through self-compassion, you access a center where you can rest in comfort. It is the knowing that you have done what you could, based on the limited resources you have. You are now at your service in the embrace of support, encouragement and love.

You understand what it means to be human. You realize that

your suffering will continue so long as there is something that you are not completely satisfied with. You realize that desires do not cause suffering, but the attachment to your desires do. Through self-compassion, you become present to your suffering. You see your dreams and disappointments, hopes and failures and successes and failures. Instead of suppressing your negative emotions like you have always done, you now feel the full extent of your vulnerability, sorrow and pain.

Practicing self-compassion allows you to loosen your tight grip on craving for things in a certain way or wanting perfection. Self-compassion is the antidote that you apply when you have been too harsh in your expectations. You relax in wanting control or striving for perfection – goals that are unattainable. Through surrendering your desire for control to God/The Universe/Divine Presence, you allow yourself some space to simply be.

Developing compassion for others seems natural. When someone else is in trouble, you find yourself moved into action immediately because you are feeling compassionate. Self-compassion, on the other hand, appears to be more of a choice. Being kind to yourself is not something that you are in the habit of doing. As an important aspect towards greater self-love, it is perhaps time to make a start.

The compassion that you extend to yourself comes from the same well of unconditional love that you extend to others. You would ultimately realize that you have so much more to give only after you have practiced self-compassion. Through tapping into your inner reservoir of love, you begin to feel more alive. You learn to make peace with all the conflicts you feel on the inside.

How to Practice Self-Compassion

Embrace Yourself Unconditionally. Self-compassion is love healing, grounded in the present. It is a state of embrace. You love yourself unconditionally, wholeheartedly and fully. You forgive yourself even if you have made a mistake. Self-compassion is your warm chicken soup, soft pink blanket, cuddly teddy bear, and hot chocolate on a cold rainy day.

Let Go of Labels. Like a broken recorder in your mind, you have played the tape of labels until you are blue in the face. Labels are names or forms of identification that you have attached yourself with; such as stupid, useless, worthless, failure, lousy, unsuccessful, freak and so on. Since your self-talk is mostly negative, the labels that you have been using on the self are likely to be derogatory.

The less you hold on to labels, the more life can flow through you. When you let go of labels, you no longer restrict your appreciation of the moment by a set of narrow descriptions. You become free to explore what-is. Because your mind has been freed of clutter, it now has the space to hold your experience. Thus, your presence expands in the present moment fully and your capacity to be in appreciation of the moment increases.

Use Supportive Words. To be compassionate is to be encouraging. Your self-talk has a positive resonance. Instead of bashing yourself repeatedly, you use supportive words. You treat the self as your own best friend. This means having the ability to lift your own spirit even when things do not turn out right or turn out ideally. While the support of external parties can help, you are able to access your inner resources to feel okay about yourself. You develop inner strength.

<u>Change Your Perception.</u> You make the choice to see yourself from a more positive lens. Hence, you refuse to jump to conclusions. If your golf coach tells you that you have swung the wrong way, he or she does not mean that you are a failure. It just means that to win, you need to change the way you swing. Thus, instead of saying that you are "hopeless at golf", you learn to swing the right way. And so, you keep improving your swings until you can do them well.

<u>Release Attachment To Yardsticks.</u> To be compassionate is to give up being "right" or "wrong". You become less attached to a fixed view of the world. You also refuse to judge yourself using other people's standards. You recognize that the standards of others may not necessarily apply to you. To impose these yardsticks would be unfair to you.

Turn Self-Criticism to Self-Compassion

Notwithstanding, note that there is nothing wrong with doing some form of appraisal. If you cannot be honest with yourself, who can you be honest with? Also know that avoidance in looking at your own faults is a form of self-delusion. You delude yourself into believing that there is nothing wrong with you, when what you are experiencing on the inside is chaos.

Only when you do self-evaluation can you be aware of your insecurities, sadness, anger, resentment, and so on. With awareness, you create the opportunity for release. As Buddha says, "A day spent judging another is a painful day. A day spent judging yourself is a painful day." You let go of the negative emotions that have been keeping you from living a full life.

No one can possibly understand your pain more than

yourself. And hence, healing is best done for the self by the self. Self-compassion facilitates healing through acceptance, forgiveness, kindness, and understanding. You treat your raw wounds tenderly. This also means not trying to cover up or fix anything, but observe your wounds as they-are, without judgment.

There are probably many things that you have done that you are not proud of. However, you will also realize that your behavior do not make you bad, wrong or evil. More likely, you have reacted the way you did because somewhere in your subconscious is the resonance of fear. Self-compassion opens the door to clarity. You now understand more about your life lessons. You are to learn about shifting out from fear-based emotions.

The practice of self-compassion is important in order to heal the emotional wounds of feeling separate. While others can show you compassion, the most powerful healing comes from being able to love yourself. Divine essence springs from within. Self-compassion allows you to experience the truth of your being.

Fear is a thought in your mind. Compassion is the love in your heart. Each time you are ready to judge, you are feeling the separation away from your true self or Source. You experience fear. However, each time you let go of the judgment or criticism, your heart heals. Your healing thereby contributes to the elevation of human consciousness, since you are part of universal oneness.

Indeed, father of modern physics, Albert Einstein, once said...

"A human being is a part of a whole, called by us 'universe,' a part limited in time and space. He experiences himself, his thoughts and feelings as something separated from the rest... a

kind of optical delusion of his consciousness. This delusion is a kind of prison for us, restricting us to our personal desires and to affection for a few persons nearest to us. Our task must be to free ourselves from this prison by widening our circle of compassion to embrace all living creatures [including ourselves!] and the whole of nature in its beauty."

Negative Self-Talk Pattern #5: Neglect

It's okay. My needs can wait.
Self-care sounds selfish. I don't want to come across as self-centered.
I will only see the doctor when my condition turns critical.
No one notices me anyway, so I am happy not to dress up.
I am too busy to take a break.
Sleep is a waste of time.

A lack of self-love increases the tendency for neglect. You refuse to attend to your basic needs such as regular meals, appropriate clothing or personal hygiene. Even when you are sick, you refuse to take time for needed rest. You are always up and about – with no requests for downtime. Thus, self-neglect can lead to reduced attempts in having a holistic lifestyle. You do not exercise, eat unhealthily and are not motivated to be well.

Understandably, it can be easy to let things slide when you are busy. You are desperately trying to play catch-up. Time, you realize, is a scarce resource. And so you neglect things that you feel that you can always come round to. The problem is that you never get to them. These items get pushed further and further down in your priority list. And they are important activities like having adequate sleep, meditation, showing up for routine doctor appointments and so on.

At the extreme, you even totally sacrifice your own needs. There is no doubt that you find it easier to place the needs of others way above yours. You like knowing that you make a difference to the lives of others. Thus, you are ever ready to help, even if it means resulting in your inconvenience. However, when you consistently place your own needs last, you set the stage for exhaustion, resentment and a feeling of being unfulfilled. You just do not feel well.

Loving Yourself Through Self-Care

"Self-development is a higher duty than self-sacrifice."
- Elizabeth Cady Stanton

It is important to realize that self-care is anything but selfish. In fact, it is essential. Just like breathing. Self-care qualifies as physiological needs. Physiological requirements, according to famous psychologist Abraham Maslow, lie at the bottom of a pyramid of a typical person's needs. All other needs, such as self-esteem, are secondary until physiological requirements are fulfilled.

Basic self-care involves taking care of your physical needs such as food, water and shelter. However, holistic self-care should also extend to addressing your spiritual and emotional needs. You engage in activities that bring overall wellness. It means developing the ability to discern when to say yes and when to say no to requests. However, once you have decided that the answer is no, you do not allow guilt to take over.

When you look after yourself, you become more relaxed, patient, fulfilled and happier. You are well from the inside. Everyone benefits when you feel well. Others like being near you as you have now become more fun to be with. Your light-heartedness is infectious. They feel encouraged to be the same way.

Ways to Self-Care

There are many ways that you can undertake self-care. Here are some of my favorite mind-body-spirit ways....

Exercise Regularly. Regular exercise gets neglected if you lead a sedentary lifestyle with little physical activity. Sedentary activities usually include sitting, watching television and computer use for hours without you removing your butt off the chair. You already ought to know that exercise improves your mood, wards off diseases and cope with stress. Adults should do a minimum of 30 minutes moderate-intensity physical activity, five days a week.

Eat a Healthy Balanced Diet. Having a balanced diet means choosing a wide variety of foods, ensuring that you have adequate nutrients from all the food groups. It involves eating certain things in moderation; namely saturated fat, trans fat, cholesterol, refined sugar, salt and alcohol. Eating healthily means making responsible food choices for your overall wellness.

Have Adequate Sleep. Getting adequate sleep should not be perceived as a time-wasting activity. It is impossible for your body to keep going if you do not have sufficient sleep. Sleep is absolutely necessary for the regulation of your hormones and body processes. You are less likely to fall ill, when you have slept enough and well. Adults need an average of 8 hours of sleep, although this can vary from person to person. What is more important is getting quality sleep than a night of restless tossing in bed.

<u>Drink Sufficient Water Daily.</u> Loving your body involves ensuring that you have sufficient water intake. Drinking enough water is needed to combat dehydration. When you are dehydrated, you have less energy, cannot concentrate as well and feel generally more tired. What is recommended is the standard "eight glasses a day" of water, which equates to two litres.

<u>Take a Break.</u> Just because you are taking a break does not mean that you are committing a heinous crime. Learn to say no if you need some time and attention for yourself. There is no need to feel guilty for taking me-time. Feeling tired? Take an afternoon nap or sleep in. Or consider going on a vacation break for a couple of days.

<u>Remove Physical Clutter.</u> Having excessive physical clutter around can weigh you down. Clear your desk to make some space. Consider throwing away things that can no longer be used. And most certainly, give away your old clothes to the needy. Get to experience an invigorating lightness after a spring-cleaning exercise.

<u>Let Go of Emotional Clutter.</u> The idea is not about being putting yourself in pain. Rather it is to review areas in your life that is causing you unhappiness, stress and conflict. Spend an afternoon, night or simply allocate some time to clear emotional clutter. Use self-help techniques like Emotional Freedom Technique (please see later chapter on its explanation).

<u>Make a To-Do List.</u> If you have been feeling overwhelmed, sit down and make a list of to-do things, ranking them in priority. Getting your tasks down on paper gives you a clearer idea of what is or is not essential. You experience greater clarity and become more focused.

<u>Get Help.</u> If you are finding things hard to cope, ask for help. Do not be shy or be afraid to request for assistance. No one will know that you are facing difficulties if you do not make utter a word about feeling overwhelmed. As the famous saying goes, "Ask and you shall receive". Learn to set aside your fear of rejection and ask for assistance appropriately.

<u>Connect with Nature.</u> Whether you go to the beach to enjoy the sea breeze or walk in a park of smiling orchids, connecting with nature helps in the rejuvenation of your spirit. Be fully present. Be aware of the energy that weaves through you and the rest of nature. Experience a sense of comfort, nurture and peace in the embrace of Mother Earth.

Turn Self-Neglect to Self-Care

Self-care is nourishing your inner home. Just like in a physical home, you need to keep your inside clean, comforting and safe. Hence, you do not wreck yourself apart when you undertake self-care. This means that you do not give excuses for feeling tired, crying or going for a snooze. You do not have to be in a rush to explain yourself to anyone.

Self-care may mean eating more, less or having a treat every now and then. Whatever it is, you take a balanced approach to overall holistic well-being. You take reasonable pride in looking good and you cultivate a positive mental attitude. During challenging periods, you give yourself some space for downtime. You allow yourself enough time to grieve, heal and rejuvenate.

It is important to schedule time for self-care. If you schedule time to meet everyone else's needs, you have to do the same for yourself too! Setting aside time requires some concerted effort. If you have been neglecting yourself, it is possible that you feel reluctant in having to break your usual routine of putting your own needs last.

But it is worth it! After you have practiced self-care for a while, taking me-time becomes something natural. You will discover that you cannot do without it! Hence, give yourself the permission to undertake self-care. Make your wellness a top priority. You feel more alive when you flourish from the well-tended garden of your soul.

The ultimate self-care is taking steps to nurture yourself in every way possible. Because your soul is innately creative, find ways to nurture yourself creatively. It may mean dancing, painting, sculpturing, designing some new software or coming up with innovative solutions. Self-nurture allows your soul to flourish, beyond fulfilling your basic physical needs. You are in the flow when you are engaged in these creative activities. Ultimately, you are channeling divine love, which seeks to express itself through your being.

Negative Self-Talk Pattern #6: Denial

I do not have any problems.
I do not need support.
My dreams are not important.
My needs are not important.
I deny my love for dancing.
My passion does not make me money.
I do not feel deprived.

When you are in denial, you are not being truthful to yourself. Self-denial puts you in a state of contradiction, conflict and restraint. You deliberately control your own natural instincts by refraining from any self-indulgence.

Unwilling to honor your true feelings, you do not give yourself the permission to be authentic.

There can be some overlap but there is a slight nuance to self-neglect and self-denial. Self-neglect is when you do not take care of your own needs whereas self-denial is when you do not even acknowledge that you have specific or unique needs. When you are in self-denial, you are in neglect. You cannot admit to having issues. And so, you put on the facade that all is well and try to shoulder the burden alone. You find it shameful to appear helpless.

Denial arises from the inner sense of lack. Hence, you deny or starve yourself of love. Even though you are often generous with others, you refuse to do the same for yourself. You heap praises and encouragement on others but have nothing good to say to the self. Ironically, you expect the same validation from others because you fear being forgotten or overlooked. While it seems as if you are willing to help others generously, you actually have expectations of some kind of payoff.

Self-denial is Cinderella's story. Cinderella had initially resigned herself to serving the needs of her two step-sisters and step-mother. Magic only happened when she decided to ask for what she wanted. Miraculously, her fairy godmother appeared to grant her the wish of going to a Royal Ball. Cinderella got what she desired when she acknowledged her own needs.

The childhood message that probably has the most immense impact on you is that it is not okay to have your own unique needs. You have been encouraged to conform. You are encouraged to suppress your own dreams because of perceived societal threats of non-acceptance. However, as humans, it is instinctual to have needs. Not only that, each one of us is unique with needs and dreams that can differ from others.

Assisting others, especially at the expense of the self, can appear to be a noble thing at first. You are a hero in the eyes of your family and friends. Consequently, they believe that they can count on you to show up, as you have always done. However, excessive self-denial robs you of vital life energy. You suffer in the long run. Gradually, you wear yourself down.

Loving Yourself Through Self-Honesty

> "The worst education which teaches self-denial, is better than the best which teaches everything else, and not that." – John Sterling

The opposite of being in denial is to be honest. Self-honesty means being authentic. You are willing to be true, stand up to your values and say yes to your inner being. When you are authentic, you are nurturing and celebrating your uniqueness. You move beyond mere self-acceptance to nourishing your being to wholeness.

Saying yes to yourself may mean that you have to say no to others. Undertaking self-nurture is often a misunderstood to mean being selfish. Having the mistaken belief, you experience guilt if you should say "no" to others. Even if it means sacrificing your own needs, you feel compelled to agree to an unreasonable request of your time and energy.

However, guilt is an energy that tears at your heart. It has a negative resonance. You feel obliged to give from an already leaking tank. Because your tank is getting empty, you need to find a way to refuel yourself. It becomes possible that you hope that whatever service you render to others will be responded to in return.

Convinced of being unlovable, denial can lead you to becoming covertly needy of care and affection from others. Obviously, others are unaware that you are in greater need of care and affection than you seem to need. After all, you have been presenting the front that everything is okay. There are times when you feel afraid to ask for what you need. Yet, there are other times when you assume that others ought to know what your needs are. Invariably, unmet expectations can cause you much unhappiness. You are led to conclude that you are not good, worthy or lovable enough.

Authenticity often demands repeated affirmation. You will be presented with enough trials and tribulations for you to align with your true self. Amazingly, each time you say yes to yourself, new and unexpected options will open up. Miracles unfold by your decision to honor what your heart tells you. Do not take my word for it, though. Just answer the call to greater authenticity and see what happens.

How to Practice Authenticity

Cultivate Courage. It appears to be easier to deny than to be honest. Your forte is sweeping things under the carpet. At the most, when things go wrong, you can point the blame at others. Denial is shirking responsibility for the self. You avoid meeting the truth in your heart.

Authenticity requires courage. It means standing up for your true self. You have the courage to speak up, act and behave according to your inner values. You are honest about your own specific needs. Courage is needed because facing the truth can sometimes be a painful process.

The intent for authenticity can possibly involve taking an unconventional path. Conformity with what others want is no longer the top priority as compared to being in alignment with your inner truths. Hence, it means cultivating the courage to make different decisions and chart out a unique course for yourself.

Go on a Self-Discovery Journey. Loving yourself requires you to know yourself intimately. It involves time, dedication and persistence. Through self-discovery, you will be led to amazing truths about yourself. It may appear to be painful in the beginning but pain, being an illusion, disappears with emerging realization. Eventually, you will find that it is not possible to not love the self that you are at the core.

I encounter many people who claim that they have no idea who they are and what they truly want in life. However, I believe that rather than giving up or staying confused, it is important to search for answers. Going on a self-discovery journey is necessary. When questions are held in the mind, the subconscious will start to draw the resources and information needed for deriving answers.

Say Yes to your Dreams. Perhaps you are one of the lucky few, who already know what your dreams are. However, you refuse to pursue them out of fear. You are scared that your ideas will not accepted, that it is difficult to make money from living your passion or that others may disapprove of you.

Saying yes to your dreams does not mean that you act foolishly. It does not necessarily mean that you quit your job immediately in a new pursuit. However, it does mean finding a way to bring your gifts, talents and strengths together to cultivate a dream that brings an added-value contribution to people. The greater your ability to do so, the more people you will serve, the more fun you will have and the more money you will make. But first, align with the passion to carry your dreams through. You will invariably be passionate by virtue of being authentic to your true desires.

Turn Self-Denial to Self-Honesty

Instead of being in denial, lay claim to who you are. Loving yourself means taking ownership with everything that is about you. You are honest with yourself and you no longer seek to hide your truth from others. Thus, you make no apologies or give no excuses for being you.

If it means losing some friends, you know that you will be fine. You no longer crave for the acceptance of these friends. It is possible to find them becoming clingy or demand that you do not change. However, be aware of the need to let go of old energies that are no longer in vibrational match with the direction that you wish to go. Hence, you become confident of drawing a new set of friends and circumstances that support the new you. You stay firm in the transition for a transformational breakthrough.

Being authentic allows you to take charge of your dreams. You no longer deny their existence. You are honest with yourself that they matter. You are honest with yourself that you matter. While it helps to get advice from others, you are cognizant that you make the final call. Thus, you do not drown out your own voice. Because you are authentic, you cannot be any happier. Inadvertently, you set the ground for self-love.

Negative Self-Talk Pattern #7: Doubt

I doubt that I can do it.
I am just too old to learn at my age.
I have always been a slow learner.
I am not intelligent enough.
I don't trust that I can make my own decisions.
No matter what I do, I will never be as good as him.
I am fearful of making mistakes.
I dislike having to make big decisions.
It is hard for me to trust others.

Every one simply believes in you. They think that you are great, loyal and responsible. You also produce excellent work. You show great potential. Hence, they are led to think that if you keep doing what you are doing, you are likely to meet with success. They demonstrate their support by cheering, "You can do it!"

The problem is that you are not able to share the same opinion about yourself. You are deluged with doubt. Highly suspicious, you do not trust that you are all that capable. Others are too kind, you say. Self-doubt happens when you have little belief in the self. You are plagued with insecurity.

Doubt drags you down with worry. Worrying puts your mind in the future. Even though there is no way of knowing what is going to happen, you are already predicting a picture of doom. A state of constant worry causes you to experience an energy leakage. You are more apt to complain about things, compare yourself with others and less likely to be rational. Your relationships with others get affected as a result.

Take attractive-looking Celeste, for instance. She was a former air stewardess. By the time 40-year-old Celeste came to see me, she was suffering from anxiety attacks because of her incessant insecurity. When queried, Celeste acknowledged that she did not actually have any grounds for suspicion. Apparently, her husband's only "fault" was that he was a good-looking guy who was often away on business trips.

Celeste became anxious because recent newspaper articles reported an alarming increase of cases of infidelity. She became more and more worked up, just thinking of how easy it would be for her husband to have an extra-marital affair. During the discussion, Celeste started to blame her husband for causing her so much doubt; which led to her distrust. She also admitted to having a strained relationship in the recent weeks because she would find fault with her husband over the smallest thing. Her worry was also causing her to lose sleep.

Celeste was led into realizing that she needed to look inwards. At the heart of her insecurity with her husband was the lack of self-trust. Worry was letting her know that she was out-of-alignment. She did not trust that she was "good enough" for her husband to stay faithful to her. There have also been many indications of the lack of self-trust on her part in other areas of her life, including the inability to make small decisions and to take risks.

It was a moment of awareness for Celeste. She realized instead of blaming and worrying over something that might or might not happen, she was far better off working on her self-trust. Her husband was only projecting her issues on trust. Most of all, Celeste understood that she needed to love herself, instead of neglecting her own physical needs. There were unresolved childhood issues that she needed to look into.

Doubt displaces. You lose your center. Your mind is always

sometime in the future. You lose the capacity to experience life in the here and now. In excessive worry, you deny yourself the opportunity of living your moments in freedom. Life seems tedious when you have to live with insecurity and be constantly on the lookout. You are unable to rest in peace. You get easily overwhelmed when you need to analyze your various options. Consumed by the fear of making a wrong decision, you keep turning to others for their opinions.

Self-doubt causes you to cling on to things that you believe are dependable. However, you eventually find out that nothing in the physical world is one hundred percent secure. Thus, you are unable to feel grounded. It becomes hard to love yourself when you are perpetually feeling anxious. Your mind is just too preoccupied with the fear in your mind, to connect with the love in your heart.

Steeped in doubt, you also believe that you do not have adequate resources to help you cope with life. And so you are always in a constant strife to seek outside factors such as systems, ideas and people to provide you with the support. Even then, you doubt in your ability to receive assistance from others or the universe. Notwithstanding, when assistance is rendered to you, you become suspicious on whether others are hoping for something back in return.

Doubt blocks the connection to your intuition. You have trouble listening to your own inner guidance. On the extreme, you can become clingy, dependent and needy. Extremely anxious to please everyone, you crave for consensus before you are able to make a small decision. It often feels like you need a long time to deliberate before you arrive at a clear decision. Invariably, self-doubt leads you to losing much inner power.

The childhood message that you probably have received is

that you need to exercise restraint lest you look silly, that you should never question your parents or that you were too sensitive. As protective parents, they believe that they know better. Your parents were very anxious about you making mistakes. They did not want you to suffer negative consequences. Thus, everything was decided for you. Furthermore, they were concerned that they might "lose face".

As it turned out, there have been few opportunities to learn how to make decisions. You have simply accepted and obeyed your parents, caregivers or any figures of authority. Over time, you lose the willingness to explore, dare or dream because you find yourself experiencing continual self-doubt. Self-doubt can also make it hard for you to claim your accomplishments. You cannot give yourself credit when due. There is little belief that you have got what it takes to succeed.

Doubt is the voice of the ego. Your ego wants to keep you safe, in your comfort zone. It derives no joy with you taking a risk. It does not want you on the roller coaster ride in the theme park. It does not want you to go mountain climbing. Doubt stops you from going on adventures. It claims that there is too much at stake from looking like a failure. So it prevents you from taking any chance at all. Doing anything new or different is just too risky.

Unfortunately, once you start to pay attention, the voice of doubt only gets louder and louder. Doubt is fear in your mind. It stifles the dream in your heart. Again and again, you are not able to move purposefully in the direction of your dream. Even where you have started on working towards your dream, excessive self-doubt can cause you to abandon things prematurely.

I have wanted to write a book on Self-Love for sometime. However, I did not believe that I could. Sure, it would be okay to write a few pages but to write a book on Self-Love sounded daunting at first. At one stage, the more I thought about writing the book, the more doubt I had. Doubt begged me not to waste my time. It pleaded, scolded and cajoled.

Soon, a debate started to take place between the voice of doubt and that of my heart. Fortunately, my heart won. I had felt moved by the emails written by my readers that I had been receiving daily for three years. The book would answer questions likely to be posed by anyone facing difficulties with self-love.

I finally became convinced that this would be the perfect book to write because it would help me with greater insights. After all, I needed to practice more self-love myself. At this point, it also dawned on me what strong doubt could possibly do. It was definitely insane of me to compare my work with the very best of authors. What was I thinking? I will just do the best I can. I will start writing from what I know and allow the rest to unfold on its own. As it turned out, what began as a few pages soon became a book.

So yes, I understand what it must be like for you when you think about pursuing your dream. While most people do suffer from self-doubt pangs every now and then, a severe case of insecurity can stop you in your tracks. And so you find it hard to succeed. It is important to recognize that even happy or successful people have their doubts. They are just better at focusing what they want and they follow up with massive action behind their goals.

Loving Yourself Through Trust

"Focus more on your desire than on your doubt, and the dream will take care of itself. You may be surprised at how easily this happens. Your doubts are not as powerful as your desires, unless you make them so."
- Marcia Wieder

You want to be free to explore life but doubt holds you back. You do not trust that you have the ability to cope with change. Hence, you try to stay within your own comfort zone. Holding on to safety creates a false sense of security because there can be nothing that is absolutely unshakeable. Doubt can keep you stuck after a while. To go forward, you will need to overcome doubt and learn self-trust.

Because doubt is a creation in your mind, only you can remove its seed. Depending on others to clear your doubt can be helpful but nothing beats cultivating the trust from within. The more you believe in yourself, the easier it becomes in boosting your sense of self-worth. You gain strength. As Henry Ford said, "Whether you think you can, or think you can't, you're right."

To start gaining self-trust, summon courage. Summoning courage does not mean wishing for the absence of fear. Courage is the spurt of energy that motivates you into action, even in the presence of fear. A gathering momentum of strength dissolves the energy of doubt once you kick into gear. It may not be anything big that you are attempting to do. What is more important is that you are letting go of the known to venture anew. In fact, the more times you break down doubt, the greater your ability to cultivate self-trust.

Role Models of Success

The following are well-known examples of people who have succeeded against all odds. Not allowing the first signs of obstacles to deter them, they learned to overcome self-doubt. What is remarkable was that many of them were initially told by their detractors that they did not have what it takes to make it. However, they did not let their initial disappointment stop them from trying again and again; until they succeeded.

Thomas Edison. Thomas Edison was an American inventor who developed many life-changing devices such as the phonograph and the light bulb. As a prolific inventor, he had more than 1,000 U.S patents to his name.

However, when he was young, teachers told him that he was "too stupid to learn anything". In school, the young Edison's mind often wandered. He only lasted 3 months. He was eventually homeschooled by his mother.

Edison was also hearing impaired. It is ironic that he would eventually be involved in the development of the motion picture camera. For developing the light bulb to great commercial success, he was most famous for the following quote...

"I have not failed. I've just found 10,000 ways that won't work."
- Thomas Edison

Michael Jordan. Michael Jordan is known as the greatest basketball player of all time. His persistence paid off after he failed to make it for the varsity basketball team during his sophomore year. At 5'11" (1.80 m) back then, he was deemed too short to play at that level.

Instead of pouting or making excuses over failure, Jordan practiced hard at perfecting his game. His burning desire to win, coupled with his utter refusal to quit, made him a legend in his time.

"Obstacles don't have to stop you. If you run into a wall, don't turn around and give up. Figure out how to climb it, go through it, or work around it." - Michael Jordan

<u>J.K. Rowling.</u> The original Harry Potter and the Philosopher's Stone was rejected by a dozen publishers; including big houses like Penguin and Harper Collins. Bloomsbury, a small London publisher, only took it because the CEO's eight-year old daughter begged her father to print the book.

Before Rowling wrote the Harry Porter series, she was in poverty, severely depressed and a single parent. She went from depending on welfare to being one of the richest women in the world in a span of only five years through hard work and perseverance.

> *"Failure meant a stripping away of the inessential. I stopped pretending to myself that I was anything other than what I was, and began to direct all my energy into finishing the only work that mattered to me. Had I really succeeded at anything else, I might never have found the determination to succeed in the one arena I believed I truly belonged. I was set free, because my greatest fear had already been realised, and I was still alive, and I still had a daughter whom I adored, and I had an old typewriter and a big idea. And so rock bottom became the solid foundation on which I rebuilt my life." - JK Rowling*

<u>Elvis Presley.</u> His manager, Jimmy Denny, told him, "You ain't

goin' nowhere, son. You ought to go back to drivin' a truck."

<u>Harrison Ford.</u> In his first ever film, Harrison Ford was told by movie execs that he did not have what it would take to be a star.

<u>Ludwig van Beethoven.</u> His teachers thought that he was hopeless and that he would never succeed as a composer or at the violin.

Then, there have been also countless other inspiring models like the Wright Brothers, Oprah Winfrey, Charlie Chaplin, Donald Trump, Winston Churchill and so on, who succeeded.

Turn Self-Doubt to Self-Trust

One night, while I was writing this book, I had a dream. In my semi-conscious state, I was commanded by a voice to write this dream down in my book. So here was how the dream went: There was a snail with a big dream. Its dream was to travel the world. The snail told the other animals about its dream. However, the other animals jeered at it. They felt that it was too impossible to achieve. The cheetah said, "There is no way it can go round the world. It is far too slow!"

Despite the taunts, the snail decided to proceed anyway. It went on a path that took him around the world. Because the snail could only move at its own pace, it took a long time. It could not be rushed. However, it persisted in its dream because it had held on to its belief: *slow and steady wins the race*. The snail finally made it.

The thought of a giant step towards self-trust may seem daunting; hence, begin by making small steps. You gain self-trust with the benefit of experience. While courage helps you get started, you will need persistence. Persistence offers you the resilience to break down the barricades of doubt. Work your way up gradually. Metaphorically speaking, it is like making your way up a ladder. To climb the rungs of a ladder, you first need to let go of doubt that keeps you stuck on the lower steps. Each higher rung climbed helps you gain in confidence.

To learn self-trust, listen to the voice of your intuition. Your intuition is the heart's inner wisdom. It is your sixth sense. Admittedly, I have often experienced confusion with this question: How do I know whether the voice comes from my ego or my intuition? When I needed to make a choice over a few options, I had a hard time discerning between the two voices. Then, gradually, I became more aware of the distinction.

Here was what I found out. When you are in touch with the intuitive voice of your heart's wisdom, you experience a sense of peace. There is no internal conflict. On the other hand, drama is present when it comes from your ego. It does not come from a place of love. Rather, it comes from a space of fear. Being driven by emotions is not the same thing as being guided by feelings. Emotions are egotistical reactions, whereas feelings are the intuitive whispers from the wisdom of your heart.

As you lose your anxieties, you will naturally feel supported by the benevolence of the universe. There is faith that you will never be short on divine assistance. Spirit is everywhere. It is in the flowers, trees, sky, stars, friends, family, pebbles, birds and bees. You are spirit too, except that you are currently in human form. With increasing awareness, you become more centered. You relax into a state of grounded openness. And it is from here, that you come into the acceptance that you are as worthy as anyone else in the universe.

Negative Self-Talk Pattern #8: Pity

Poor me! I am ill fated.
Why does this always happen to me?
Why are others so much luckier than I am?
I have few friends. No one supports me.

Self-pity seems comforting when you are feeling lousy. You go through your "poor me" stories like a mantra. There is no denying that you enjoy the attention that your pity parties bring. You perceive that self-pity allows you to better elicit a loving response from others. Yearning for sympathy, you hope that others will feel sorry for you too.

In the stage of life, there had been numerous occasions when I welcomed playing the role of the victim. Self-pity provided me with a blanket of safety. It allowed me to wallow in my sorrow. Poor me, I would wet my pillow with tears. I was the main star in my own soap opera. The melodrama would grow in proportion with the level of my misery.

What got me to self-pity in the first place? I used to believe that rejection was the worst thing that could happen to me. In some ways, it could be worse than death itself. And so, I indulged myself with excessive amounts of soaked tissue paper whenever I got rejected. Ironically, over time, I grew tired of being in the starring role of my own drama. I got sick of hearing my own stories of limitation, misery and frustration.

I started daring myself in ways that help me grow in self-confidence. Each time, I challenged myself with trying things a little different.   I went on mini confidence-building adventures. I would put myself in situations where I face bigger and bigger fears. Amazingly, I discovered greater freedom with each time I make an attempt. I became lighter, more positive and willing to take risks.

As I took greater charge over my destiny, I threw fewer and fewer pity parties. They were no longer as enjoyable. I found them less and less of a celebration. On review, I realize that self-absorption can be paralyzing. It is possible for anyone to get mentally overpowered while trudging in solitary wilderness. The result is losing a grip on reality, because the story in the inner landscape has proven to be more engaging.

I have since recognized that rejection is a part of life. It is inevitable. Everyone is likely to have experienced rejection at one point in his or her life. What is more is that by looking at some of the world's successful role models, I saw that they overcame periods of rejection to be the people they are today. Therefore, what is more crucial is about developing the ability to cope and manage challenges.

Self-pity invariably leads you to making comparisons about how you are doing against others. Deeming yourself as unworthy, you find that you can never measure up. It is hard to feel positive if you believe you are not good enough. Making comparisons becomes a never-ending cycle that puts you in great suffering.   You also accumulate enough "evidence" to prove that the whole world is conspiring against you.

It is hard to shift your victim mentality so long as you hold on to your misperceptions. You are not willing to consider an alternative point of view. Over time, self-pity becomes a habit that is hard to break. Wising up, your friends get tired of hearing the same story of limitation too. And you wonder why those who used to be supportive do not turn up at your pity parties any more?

All pity parties have to come to an end someday, or you will find it difficult to move forward in life. If you choose to believe that you are helpless, the universe will support you in that belief. What you reinforce in your inner self-talk becomes true in your reality. There is much wisdom to the warning, "Be careful what you wish for".

So no more drinking yourself silly late into the nights, wearing extra black mascara, gorging on comfort foods like chips or chocolate, playing sad songs such as "All Out of Love" repeatedly or other irrational behaviors to "drown your sorrows". If this has been going on for a period, it is time to stop. Make a firm resolution to. You will be thankful that you did.

Loving Yourself Through Self-Empowerment

> *"Self-pity is easily the most destructive of the non-pharmaceutical narcotics; it is addictive, gives momentary pleasure and separates the victim from reality." – John W Gardner*

Self-pity is a mask for emptiness. You are trying to make up for the hollowness you feel inside. While it feels warm and comforting at first, the problem is that self-pity can keep you trapped. Self-pity is a futile process that does not benefit you in the long run. Locked in your own prison, you dwell in pessimism, misery, depression, and regret.

Perhaps, having wallowed in a cocktail of negative feelings, you find it difficult to see how it is possible to take charge. You feel powerless. You are unable to see that you have the ability to create a different life for yourself. While grieving is important for recovery, prolonged self-pity is not healthy. Feeling safe in the cocoon of your stories, you are not likely to be motivated to make needed changes.

Most certainly, it is very healthy to be compassionate to the self. However, compassion and pity towards the self is not the same thing. Pity keeps us in a negative emotional state and stuck in the past, whereas compassion is a positive nurturing state, inviting us to live in the present. With awareness, we will see that self-pity merely provides us with a false sense of comfort. We are kept in a negative state and we can never get out to truly feeling better.

Self-pity can lead a person to addiction. If you discover that you have fallen out of love with someone else, it is possible for you to walk away. However, if you do not love yourself, your coping mechanism will want to devise an escape. The mental escape is from the things that you detest in the self. And so in a state of overwhelming self-pity, you turn to drinking, smoking or compulsive eating. The addictive behavior masks the torturous pain.

You have certainly not been born with self-pity as a gene. You honed your skills after acquiring the ability sometime in your life. Therefore, you have every power to unlearn this poor habit. Why not surprise everyone? Prance out of self-pity by adopting a more empowering mentality. As the late fashion editor, politician and diplomat, Millicent Fenwick, once said, "Never feel self-pity, the most destructive emotion there is. How awful to be caught up in the terrible squirrel cage of self."

How to Overcome Self-Pity

No More Stories of Drama. With self-pity, you make yourself out as the victim. A sense of self-righteousness reigns. You believe that you have every right to be the way you are because of external conditions. So you believe that everyone else should now make an allowance and practice sympathy towards your plight.

For change to happen, you need to first want to let go of your stories. In a nutshell, refuse to tolerate any more sob stories about the self. Be totally honest. Ask yourself if you will gain much by continuing in the same state. Realize that while it is okay to feel sad, it is not okay to indulge excessively in misery.

Also question if you are playing emotional games with others. Stop them if you are. The world does not owe you a living. You stand to lose friends if you engage in self-pity for far too long. It becomes self-fulfilling. The consequence is ending up alone. Just think about it. No one likes being near a person who holds pity parties throughout the whole year.

Disallow Blame. Self-blame is when you blame yourself but self-pity has the implicit implication that you are blaming some external factor, person or event. Mostly, self-blame conjures guilt but self-pity conjures sadness.

Understandably if you have suffered abuse or trauma as a child, it is easy to blame your parents for causing you to be dysfunctional. But you need to view blame as having a dateline; otherwise, your story will continue to keep you trapped.

The only way is to neutralize your emotions arising from the past. The past is gone. Hence, release the energetic imprints created by your memories. The more you are able to work through the layers of these imprints, the more freedom you are likely to experience. Gradually, you become free to love yourself as you are and to value your own being tremendously.

Stepping aside helps. Think about your parents and guardians. Understand why they have told you the negative messages. Have they been told these themselves because of their own upbringing? Have they formed these beliefs because of the traumas that they went through? How were their childhoods like? Did they also have parents who gave them a hard time?

If your parents have no awareness how to love themselves, you cannot expect them to be able to know how to love you. They have also been carrying open childhood wounds around too. To take care of you when you were young, they were doing what they could; based on the resources they had. They parented you in the only way that they knew how.

Should it be possible, have a talk with your parents about how it was like when they were young. If you listen with an open heart, you will realize that they have been once hurt badly too. When you understand what it has been like for them, you no longer blame them for saying unkind things to you. These negative thoughts had been their realities too and they probably did not realize the harm that these have caused.

Know that blame is toxic. You alienate your loved ones through blame. Hence, take some responsibility. Change your mental story from blame to one of trust and forgiveness. Not just with yourself, your relationships with others will improve for sure.

See How Far You Have Come. Through an honest assessment, see how much you have grown, matured and evolved over the years. Know that you have it in you to succeed, as long as you do not hold on to your debilitating stories. If you have succeeded in the past, use the specific memories as anchors for you in the way forward. Every time you are feeling down, call these up as reminders and for powering the belief that you can do it all over again.

Focus on Your Blessings. When you focus on your blessings, you automatically tune into joy. It is impossible to feel horrible at the same time. You are thankful instead of feeling sorry about the way you are. Make it a daily habit to express thanks for the abundance that you enjoy.

Engage in Physical Exercise. Studies show that your emotional well-being improves with physical exercise. Feel-good brain chemicals known as endorphins are released during exercise. As such, exercise has been known to help reduce depression drastically.

When I was going through an intense period of self-pity in my early 20s, I turned to physical exercise. It certainly helped keep my mind off my mental stories. I always felt better after a good workout. In other words, sweat it out to beat self-pity!

Transform Pain into Inspiration. Choose to tell a more empowering tale. The way to do this is to change your perspective by challenging long- held assumptions. Turn your story of pain into one of inspiration. Instead of your usual self-talk, you will be asking yourself, "What can I learn from my pain for a better way forward?"

Born with no legs and limbs, Nick James Vujicic is a motivational leader who demonstrates how it is possible to lead a life of no limits. He was born with Tetra-amelia, a rare disorder characterized by the absence of all four limbs. He struggled as a child, contemplated suicide at age 8 and eventually came to terms with his disability and mastered his life. He now gives talks that inspire hope, change and grace.

When you listen to his story, you will realize that you have got little to complain about. There are tons of things in your life to be grateful for. Therefore, start to pick yourself up and overcome your challenges. Be courageous and determined, rather than be known as the one stuck in self-pity for years.

<u>Have a Vision.</u> Reclaiming your dreams keeps your mind occupied with what you can do to bring it into reality. As soon as you reclaim them, you will realize that there is little or no time to waste. Letting go of self-pity automatically happens when you work towards your vision. You are far too busy putting your plans into action, than to spend time sobbing or in destructive behaviors. Every moment counts towards the building of your dream.

Turn Self-Pity to Self-Empowerment

To be self-empowered, take personal charge of your life. It means becoming inner directed. Supported by your values, you are able to make your own decisions confidently. You are also willing to accept the consequences of your actions. Thus, you become engaged with life.

Instead of being trapped in the past, choose to live in the present. You understand that only in the present well lived can there be hope for a better future. At the same time, keep an eye on your vision. No longer holding yourself back with debilitating stories, you stay focused on the picture of what you hope to create.

When you love yourself, you will want to gain mastery. Mastery starts with understanding all there is to know about yourself. Through self-discovery, it becomes possible to harness your gifts and abilities to the fullest. And you would love to be able to use them in the highest service for others. Hence, to lead a life of fulfillment, make the intent of gaining deep awareness and developing authentic alignment with who you really are.

To be self-empowered does not mean that you no longer seek assistance or require the support of others. In fact, you still do. However, you ask for help appropriately, not by way of playing the victim. You no longer operate from ego consciousness but from the alignment of your being with spirit.

It also means that you call on both seen and unseen helpers for the resources that you need in bringing your soul purpose forward. While you own your power, you also surrender it to higher intelligence that orchestrates the workings of the universe with perfect timing and order. In so doing, you acknowledge your role as a co-creator. It is how you develop magnificence.

Story: Chicken and the Eagles by Author Unknown

A long time ago in a remote valley, there lived a hardworking farmer who found the egg of an eagle from the top of a cliff. When he got home, he put the egg together with the rest of the chicken eggs in the nest that he kept in the yard.

After some weeks later, a healthy eaglet emerged from the egg. The mother hen proceeded to raise the eaglet as one of her own. The eaglet grew up with its brother and sister chicks. It learned to do all the things chickens do. It clucked and cackled. It scratched in the dirt for grits and worms. It flapped its wings furiously, flying just a few feet in the air before crashing down to earth in a pile of dust and feathers.

One day, late in its life, the eagle happened to look up at the sky. High overhead, soaring majestically and effortlessly was a powerful-looking eagle.

"What's that? cried the old eagle in awe. "It's magnificent! So much power and grace! It's beautiful!"

For a while, the old eagle thought that it bore a slight resemblance to the bird soaring above. Even though it was no longer young, it had big and strong wings; larger than the rest of the birds and chickens in the farm.

"That's an eagle", replied one of the chickens nearby, "It's the King of the Birds. It's a bird of the air... not like us in the least. We are only chickens, we are birds of the earth".

With that, they all cast their eyes downwards once more and continued digging in the dirt. The old eagle felt disappointed when it heard that. Still, it decided to believe what it was told. And so it was that the eagle lived and died a chicken... because that is all it believed itself to be.

What is this story about?

This story reminds us to claim our own destiny and not simply accept what others say who we are. It is sad that the eagle in the story died, not knowing that it was actually a majestic bird with great vision and power. Feeling powerless, it had the belief that it was small.

Chart From Self-Hatred to Self-Love

Self-rejection	Self-acceptance
I am nothing special.	I am special and I am lovable.
There is nothing lovable about me.	I accept myself for who I am.
I am such a freak. No one will ever like me. Least of all, myself.	I embrace everything about myself; including weaknesses, faults and imperfections.
I have no gifts.	I have unique qualities and gifts.
I am not capable.	I am capable and have the ability to create an amazing life for myself.
I just cannot stand my own looks.	I accept myself no matter how I look.
Self- blame	**Self-compassion**
It is my fault for things turning out this way.	I did what I could, based on the resources I had.
It is just my fault for making her angry.	I am not responsible for how she feels.

Why was I ever born? I never do things right.	My contributions are valuable. It is up to me to make things right.
Why am I such a lousy mother? I cannot even teach my children well.	I do or have done the best I can. Most importantly, I love my children very much.
I have made so many mistakes!	Everyone has made mistakes. Mistakes provide learning feedback.
I blame myself for causing the rape, trauma or abuse.	What is past is past. I can never truly know why things have come to pass in the way they have. It is now up to me to take charge of my life.
Self-deprecation	**Self-esteem**
I look down on myself.	I have positive beliefs about myself.
I am worth peanuts.	I am worthy.
I feel ashamed about myself.	I feel good about myself.
I am never good enough.	I am enough.
No matter what I do, I can never be up to scratch.	I have all that it takes to succeed in the area that matters most.

Self-criticism	Self-compassion
I am way too stupid.	Making an unwise decision does not mean I am stupid.
I am a slow learner.	Taking my time does not mean that I am slow.
What was I thinking? I will never be accepted for who I am.	I attract friends who are like-minded and who accepts and appreciates me for who I am.
It's not as if I have stellar looks. Who would take notice of me?	Looks are not everything. I have other qualities that make me lovable.
What made me say that? I feel as if I can now die a thousand deaths for looking like a fool.	Experiencing shame does not make it the end of the world. An unwise word or act does not make me who I am.
I should not have done that	There is no failure, only feedback.
I am too fat. I am too thin. I don't like my face.	I love myself no matter how I look. I love myself even though I have imperfect features.
Self-neglect	**Self-care**
It's okay. My needs can	My needs are very

	important.
wait.	
Self-care sounds selfish. I don't want to come across as self-centered.	I choose to engage in healthy self-care.
I will only see the doctor when my condition turns critical.	Health is wealth. I like to recover quickly and well.
No one notices me anyway, so I am happy not to dress up.	I like having neat appearances.

Self-denial	Self-honesty
I do not have any problems.	I acknowledge that I have some challenges.
I do not need support.	It will be great to receive some support.
My dreams are not important.	My dreams are important.
My needs are not important.	I set clear personal boundaries.
I do not feel deprived.	I would enjoy some care.

Self-doubt	Self-trust
I doubt that I can do it.	I can do this.

I am just too old to learn at my age.	Age is just a number. Learning a new skill is possible at any age.
I have always been a slow learner.	There have been times when I have learned fast.
I am not intelligent enough.	I have the keenness and ability to learn.
I don't trust that I can make my own decisions.	I trust myself. I do the best I can in making decisions and learn from my mistakes, if I have not chosen wisely.
<u>Self-pity</u>	**<u>Self-empowerment</u>**
Poor me! I am ill fated.	I create my own destiny.
Others are to be blamed for my plight.	I take responsibility for my own life.
Why are others so much luckier than I am?	There are as many unlucky people as there are lucky people. It is up to me to create opportunities for myself.
There is no way I can make it in life, from having been born into poverty.	I am able, resourceful and motivated. Where there is a will, there is a way.

Self-Talk Pattern #9: Narcissism

I am the very best and I want everyone to know that.
Let's just talk about me, me and me.
There is no one else who can ever beat my success record.
Keep your eyes on me. Watch me rise to the top.
My needs are definitely more important than everyone else's.

It can be difficult trying to distinguish between healthy self-esteem and narcissism. If you have narcissistic tendencies, you are not likely to recognize them at first. Your words, actions and behavior actually arise from fear rather than from inner strength, true confidence and positive beliefs. In the case of narcissism, you crave for attention and have an exaggerated sense of self.

You enjoy living in an invented world. With great imagination, you write an elaborate script for this world. In your script, your wildest dreams are fulfilled. Making yourself out to be some grandiose figure, you can do no wrong. After all, you have tons of adoring fans. You long to be worshipped, admired and revered. It is a world well loved by your ego.

Problems arise when you cannot separate fantasy from the real world. You project your needs of validation, love and approval in an unhealthy way. With little consideration for your family and friends, you place your needs over others. There is no doubt that you seek superiority. Superiority does well for your ego. Unfortunately, it also brings upon your own downfall. Your friends shun you after a while.

The word "narcissism" is derived from Greek mythology. Narcissus was a handsome Greek youth who was extremely proud. The Goddess Nemesis saw how he would show disdain towards those who loved him. She lured him to a pool where Narcissus saw his own reflection. Not realizing that it was simply his own image, he fell in love with his own reflection. He became besotted. Unable to leave, he lay gazing into the pool for several hours, finally changing into a flower that bears his name, the narcissus.

"Narcissism" can also be applied to more than one person simultaneously. When it is applied to a group of people, it usually denotes a sense of elitism or an indifference to the plight of other groups. Many dictators, criminals and celebrities had or have narcissistic personalities. Hitler and Stalin both had unhealthy self-images. And reportedly, so did Casanova, Marquis de Sade, and Peter Sellers.

Signs of Narcissism

Narcissism manifests in a series of signs. Ask if the following descriptions apply to you:

- You experience a high level of self-importance and behave as though your achievements are somehow bigger and better than they are in reality. You do all you can to ensure your superiority.

- You are usually preoccupied with fantasies of extreme success, power, beauty, and perfect love.

- You only seek out people who are highly ranked or who would boost your social status.

- You thrive on the admiration of others and constantly seek for it.

- You believe in your entitlement to special treatment, even though there are no reasonable grounds for any. You will not hesitate to cut queues for instance.

- You must always be the leader. You give little room for incompetency.

- You are unable to show empathy. You cannot see from the perspective of others.

- You are highly prone to jealousy.

- Your attitude is haughty towards others.

- You exploit others without apology or remorse.

Numerous books, films and television shows have narcissistic characters and/or themes. Examples of shows include: The Devil Wears Prada (Miranda Priestly role played by Meryl Streep), To Die For (Suzanne Stone role played by Nicole Kidman) and Glee (Sue Sylvester role played by Jane Lynch). The characters are shown to be prone to lying. They are portrayed as exploitative, ruthless, and opinionated as well as have inflated egos.

I also recall the story of The Emperor's New Clothes by Hans Christian Anderson, which I had read as a child. As the story goes, there lives an Emperor who is very vain. He cares for nothing but his attire. The Emperor enjoys being admired for his appearance. He likes being flattered.

One fine day, the Emperor hires two tailors who promise him the finest suit of clothes from a fabric invisible to anyone who is unfit for his position or "just hopelessly stupid". Even though the egoistic Emperor cannot see the cloth, he pretends that he can, for fear of being known to be unfit. As his ministers are also afraid of being labeled as "stupid", they pretend that they can see the fabric too. When the swindlers report that the suit is finished, they put up the appearance of dressing him up. The Emperor then marches in a street procession along with his ministers.

Suddenly, a child in the crowd blurts out that the Emperor is wearing nothing at all except for his underwear. Everyone now sees through the pretense. Suspecting that the assertion is true, the Emperor cringes. However, he holds himself up proudly and continues the procession. By then, the swindlers have made off with bags of gold as a reward for dressing the Emperor in the grandest finery; which is really nothing at all.

Shift Into Self-Awareness

What is at the very core of a narcissist is a sense of low self-love and esteem. To hide his inferiority complex, he puts up a show of pretense. His false sense of self leads to the projection of a contorted self-opinion, an erroneous worldview, and an inflated sense of being. He experiences an insatiable need to bombard others with his good points. Out of touch with his true self, he lives in an illusory world.

The irony of the situation is that a narcissist is needy of love. It may seem that he has high self-esteem but in reality, he feels unworthy. Eventually, by his own obnoxious behavior, he brings isolation upon himself. Others do not like being near him. The more he craves for attention, the more alienated he feels because he gets increasingly shunned.

Obviously, you will need to gain inner awareness if you are to spot any narcissistic tendencies in yourself. By becoming aware, you are able to catch yourself when you are playing your habitual patterns again. What will help is to stay grounded in the present moment. Being in the here and now helps you to differentiate between reality and fantasy.

Awareness holds transformational energy. You let go of the exaggerated notions of the self; which has previously been supported by hot air, empty talk and false appearances. Thus, like the Emperor in the beloved story, you become bare. At first, it can feel traumatic. However, it is through baring yourself to the world that you realize your strength. You have essentially greeted the intense fear of unworthiness by staying put, despite having nothing to show for. Fear dissolves in the process.

In your awakening, you realize that it is not always about meeting your own needs in a selfish manner. Thus, you also commit to being considerate of the needs of others. There is now genuine willingness to consult your team. No longer a pushover, you become respectful of the boundaries of others. You choose to respond with peace and love and not overreact in anger when others do not agree with your opinions. The desire to be popular, famous or superior is no longer strong.

While you are ambitious, you also act in ethical ways. You take any sign of defeat gracefully. You are able to show love and concern for others, as you are able to put yourself in their shoes. Hence, you are able to reach a level of empathy for others. You use your gifts for the good of all, instead of being self-centered. And it all starts with awareness that you are capable of loving fully and acting in a mature way.

Negative Self-Talk Pattern #10: Annihilation

I don't care about myself anymore.
It is better that I do not exist.
I am better dead than alive.
There is no place for me is this world.

I absolutely hate myself.

Self-annihilation is loathing at the most extreme. Perhaps you are already engaged in harmful addictive behavior such as heavy drinking or smoking or any form of eating disorders. Over an extended period of time, your thoughts have gotten darker and darker. You believe that your existence does not count any more and you are inclined to taking drastic measures.

Step aside to gain some perspective. Observe if you have going around carrying the energies of desperation, deep despair and destructiveness. If so, get immediate assistance. Do not dismiss your thoughts as trivial or your behavior as nothing to be concerned about. The mind is very powerful and when out of control, can lead anyone to unintentionally taking actions that are regrettable. Please do not wait to get help. Early detection can help erase the potential threat of a mishap.

Loving Yourself Through Loving Life

At the core, you have no spiritual awareness about why you are here on Earth. Your life experiences have probably sucked and so you have been feeling empty, insignificant and intrinsically unworthy. Because you do not see any meaning or purpose, you find yourself tempted to annihilate yourself.

You have no memory that your soul made the intention to be incarnated. You cannot recall saying yes to it. The truth is that your soul did make a choice. You could have stayed in the ethers but have chosen not to. Instead, your soul chose evolution; which it knew could only be possible by going through life experiences. Thus, you needed to be here physically. Unfortunately, you suffered from amnesia as soon as you were born and hence, need to reawaken your memory.

Now that you are here, realize that you have a very important decision to make. You are to choose the type of experiences you want. With choice, it is possible for you to either make your life a misery or make it an empowering one. Your choice is determined by which perspective you wish to take. If you hope to experience a turnaround, then it is important to change your lens to a more positive one. Thus, there is every need to adopt beliefs that support you in your growth. You also follow up with steps that will help you get out of the rut.

Loving life exists on the other end of the spectrum to wanting to end it. You savor every moment that puts you in touch with the feelings of joy, peace and light. Ultimately, loving life involves aligning with your higher purpose. With aligned purpose, your life becomes meaningful. Your contributions are valuable, serving the best interests of everyone concerned. At the crack of dawn, you cannot wait to get up as it means another day of living with purpose.

Reframing Your Story

Now that we have covered all the various self-talk patterns that we can possible engaged in, notice any similarity to yours so far? You may like to try doing the same exercise of recording your own self-talk over a period in order to spot patterns. Keeping a set of written records can help you to discover more about yourself.

At the time of writing this book, I found out about a meet-up group who got together for the exercise of monitoring their own individual self-talk over three weeks. During the sharing session that followed, they could not believe what one another had recorded. A number of them were taken aback when they found out that some of their more positive and optimistic-thinking members were also engaged in negative self-talk.

The inner voice of your ego is like a recording. It can affect you the whole day. You will realize that much of your self-talk robs you of your spirit and causes you to be emotionally drained. It is difficult to be well as a result. Your self-esteem gets whittled away, eroding any love that you can have for the self.

If your self-talk is negative, then learn to reframe it. "Reframing" means having an alternative point of view. It is a process that is used in Neuro-linguistic Programming to help in personal transformation. Through reframing, you alter your perspective to an empowering one. Thus, you expand your options on how you perceive the world. It means realizing that there can be more than one way of looking at things.

"Reframing" is not something unheard of when you recall the times that you have been able to look at the funny side of what appears to be a bleak situation at first. As soon as you are able to take on a more lighthearted view, your energy becomes expansive. You start to laugh. Laughter breaks your resistance from holding on to a tunnel vision.

Which reminds me of this ancient tale from China. Once there is a farmer whose horse has ran away. His neighbors are sympathetic and tell him what bad luck it is to lose a horse. The farmer responds, "maybe".

The next morning the horse returns, bringing with it three other wild horses. "How wonderful," the neighbors exclaim.

"Maybe," replies the old man. The following day, when his son attempts to ride one of the untamed horses, he gets thrown down. His son's leg gets broken.

The neighbors come over again to offer their sympathy on his misfortune. "Maybe," answers the farmer. The day after, military officials come to the village to draft young men into the army. Seeing that the son's leg is broken, they pass him by. The surprised neighbors congratulate the farmer on how well things have turned out. His response is once again "maybe."

The story shows the farmer's willingness to look at a particular situation without attachment. He does not get too hung up if things do not appear to have turned out well. He perceives the possibility that good can come out from bad experiences and that what is interpreted as positive experiences may turn out different eventually.

Reframing with Positive Affirmations

Positive affirmations are effective and beneficial tools for reframing your mind through the redirection of thoughts. Redirecting your thoughts alters your emotions immediately. Using positive affirmations especially during times of stress helps you keep your composure and balance to fend off the noise from the internal negative critic.

While reframes can produce amazing results, it must be congruent to your heart. Otherwise you will still experience an internal conflict. It is possible to feel forced into accepting that you have not already bought into. If you experience inner conflict, then cease doing affirmations until you have addressed your negative emotions or limiting beliefs.

Here are some positive affirmation statements that can be helpful for improving self-esteem:

- I am worthy of love, kindness and care.
- I am confident about life; I always long for and enjoy new challenges.
- I am a unique person and a creative individual.
- I choose to feel better about self, my work, my relationships, and every aspect of my life.
- I am actively in control of my life and I easily direct myself in productive channels.
- It is fun to be me! I enjoy getting to know myself better.
- I treat myself with utmost respect.
- I respect my values.
- I accept myself even if I have made a mistake.
- I am gracious when I receive compliments.
- I am open to receiving help and support.

Improving your mental state is not a one-day affair. You need to continually affirm positive statements especially if you wish to reprogram your mind. Reprogramming is necessary in the situation where your self-talk has been largely negative for years. Your mind has become conditioned by habit to think negatively and you need to break its patterns.

Say positive affirmations on a daily basis and see the difference that they can make to your life. One great idea is to repeat affirmations during any visioning exercises. Visioning is a process whereby you keep an eye on your desired goal or outcome. Affirmations used together with visioning can keep you on track to reaching a goal.

Reframing Your Self-Talk Story

Your self-talk is usually strung together by a series of thoughts to form a story. The negative thoughts usually feed on themselves. Gradually, you piece all the various evidence into the most incredible story. In time, you become fully convinced that you have been betrayed, treated unfairly and most of all, unloved. Thoughts repeated often enough and strengthened by emotion are known as beliefs. You also start to attract experiences that reinforce your self-talk. Thus, you become more rigid than ever in your perception of the world.

According to Abraham Hicks, spiritual beings that teach about the Law of Attraction, you can reframe your mind by telling the self better-feeling stories. You will discover that when you do so, your reality starts to change to a more positive one. When you love life, life starts loving you back. You start to attract the vibrations that match your internal paradigm. You manifest an outer world that matches your inner world.

Hence, to reframe your beliefs, look into the stories you have been telling yourself. What powered that self-talk? What beliefs did you have that came from an early childhood message? How are your emotions like as a result of your self-talk?

Recognize that you have the power to redirect your mind at any point in time. Hence, make an intention. You make the intention of loving yourself. Your desire is one of transformation because you have realized that the stories you tell yourself are not helpful. You want to put an end to the energy leakage. Telling more loving stories sound like a better idea than telling the self, painful ones.

There is no right or wrong way to tell your improved story. It can be about your past, present or future experiences. The only guideline is that it must lead you to improved feelings. Telling many good-feeling short stories throughout your day will change your point of attraction. Your internal story forms the basis of your life. So it is important to tell it the way you want things to be, rather than narrate a story of limitation – the same one you have been telling for years.

CHAPTER SIX:
SELF-LOVE - SPIRIT

*"You yourself, as much as anybody
in the entire universe, deserve your
love and affection."
- Buddha*

Understanding Root Causes

Pampering ourselves with full body massages, eating chocolate ice-cream or buying a new branded handbag are quick ways to help us relieve our stress and pain. However, to truly love the self is more than deriving satisfaction from objects of instant gratification. In fact, it is to be approached at a different level of consciousness.

As Albert Einstein said, "you can never solve the problem at the level on which it was created". While it is possible to address your self-love issues from the level of the mind or just body, you will not feel totally complete. True self-love necessarily involves your spirit. When you come to know your true nature at Source, it is impossible not to experience self-love.

Self-love is to be realized experientially. No number of books will be able to help you with deep realization until you have experienced loving yourself personally. Loving yourself has to be felt deeply from the heart. Others may tell you that you are beautiful, smart and great. However, the wounded part of your psyche will refuse to believe it. It stubbornly holds on to the beliefs that you are unworthy, unlovable or underserving. Indeed, inner work is required to process these beliefs.

Healing will be left incomplete if you are merely addressing self-love issues at the symptomatic level and not from the level of root causes. In such a scenario, you will find yourself continuing to attract the same set of circumstances that reinforce your lack. For complete healing of the cause of your wound, you will need to assimilate spiritual truths. Assimilation requires the benefit of experience, inner transcendence and physical spiritual realization through the grounding of new positive energies.

Your Life Journey

Everyone has some issues with self-love in one way or another. Ultimately, your life journey involves a reawakening into love, the source essence of your being. It is an inner discovery process. It involves the shift away from fear, which has clouded your clarity from the truth of who you are.

Experiencing contrasts help to put things into perspective. You would not be able to appreciate the truth of what-is without first experiencing the opposite. Contrast allows clarity to emerge in its fold. Just take this page that you are reading, for instance. For the words to stand out against a white background, they are best in black.

Thus, without darkness, you cannot get to know what light is. Darkness is not good or bad. It is simply the absence of light. And so it is that without first feeling separate, there would not be the impetus to know what being whole feels like. Without first feeling unworthy, you would not come to truly know what intrinsic value is.

In short, your life experiences are not good or bad. They are just meant to help you affirm or learn the truth. Problems arise when we are not aware that self-love is essentially a spiritual journey. We have grown to hate a lot of things about ourselves. It is possible to remain stuck in this negativity for years and years, when there is a lack of awareness.

On the contrary, should you gain awareness, you will realize that being in a venomous state is not the experience you truly desire. You make this realization by observing your emotions from contrasting situations. Hence, you move towards what you do want. You affirm your desire in a more positive - as in loving, joyous and peaceful – direction because you have already first come to know what you do not want.

When you do not love yourself, you are feeling disconnected. The sense of disconnection is caused by separation. You are feeling separated from others and you are feeling separated from yourself. At the core, you find it hard to own the part of you that is causing you to be ashamed, repulsed and angry. Yet, there is no escape. You are compelled to live with everything that is about you - whether you like it or not.

Should you review your past, you will realize that there are common themes to what you are currently facing. These themes can be about abandonment, rejection, betrayal, neglect, and so on. Whether they are disguised as a situation at work or home, the underlying cause can almost always be traced to a case of separation at the deepest layer.

For a long time after incarnation, you have not been aware that you are an aspect of Source. You have no idea that your essence is one and the same - love. And so you have the belief that you are separate from Source. Your belief stems from having little memory of where you came from. The stories that you tell yourself are of separation. When something happens that prevents you from knowing the presence of love, you experience the separation as fear.

You recognize fear in the form of pain, anger, resentment, sadness, addiction and worry. To deal with fear, you devise strategies to numb, sabotage, attack, deny and control. But they are all futile. Positive energy shifts can only be experienced when you start to investigate from the inside and become present to the root cause of your issues.

In reality, all you are doing is seeking reconnection with the divine source of that which you are. Everything that you say or do is an expression of fear or an expression of love. The experience of fear is indicative of separation. The experience of love is indicative of wholeness. Your life journey with its various life experiences is about integrating into wholeness.

Story: Two Wolves

There is a Native American story that has been passed down through the generations. Here it is how it goes....

An old Cherokee is teaching his grandson about life. " A fight is going on inside me," he said to the boy.

"It is a terrible fight and it is between two wolves. One is evil - he is anger, envy, sorrow, regret, greed, arrogance, self-pity, guilt, resentment, inferiority, lies, false pride, superiority, and ego." He continued, "The other is good - he is joy, peace, love, hope, serenity, humility, kindness, benevolence, empathy, generosity, truth, compassion, and faith. The same fight is going on inside you - and inside every other person, too."

The grandson thought about it for a minute and then asked his grandfather, "Which wolf will win?"

The old Cherokee simply replied, "The one you feed."

Separation from Self

We come from the same infinite Source, which is also known as God/Universe/I AM/Divine Presence. Our physical beings are an aspect of Source Energy wishing to know itself. Source Energy can only know itself experientially. It cannot know its essential nature without the benefit of experience.

It cannot truly know that itself without an experience of love or its polar-opposite, fear.

The essential nature of Source/God/Universe is love. Its qualities are compassion, warmth, support, forgiveness, strength, beauty, grace and peace. Love unites. It is of pure intelligence. It is ever-present, eternal, expansive and never-changing. Since we are Source expressed in a physical form, our basic nature is one and the same.

However, in the third dimensional world, many of us do not remember that we are all part of the same life force – the same Oneness. We have been preoccupied with keeping up with the material world that we have neglected our spiritual connection. We lead busy lives, hardly finding the time to sit down to be truly present to ourselves.

In the never-ending rush to do more and accomplish more because there is never enough, we find ourselves directing hatred, anger and frustration inwards and outwards. Hence, instead of the experience of fullness from love, peace and harmony, we experience lack. Lack is an energy very much based on fear. We feel separated. Invariably, through life experiences, conditioning and societal influences, we become out-of-alignment with who we really are.

Because we have been conditioned and ingrained by habit, it is possible to find ourselves in resistance to divine truth. We buy into misbeliefs that reside in collective consciousness. Conformity breeds a sense of comfort. We become lazy in critical-thinking. We simply assume that if everyone else says so, then it must be true. However, taking such a posture is dangerous. Growth for the self cannot happen without self-inquiry.

There are many of many beliefs in the collective

consciousness that run contrary to our true nature. Beliefs like "struggle is necessary", "I need to be perfect", "building self-confidence is dependent on having ideal body proportions" and "winning is everything" can create a lot of havoc in our lives. We create unnecessary obstacles for ourselves when we adopt these limiting beliefs. They are not true in the first place. When we fail to meet the expectations that we have set based on these beliefs, we declare war on ourselves.

Our reality is very much created and directed by our vibrational state of Being. With focused thoughts, we bring Source Energy from the unmanifested to the manifested. We can choose to manifest love or we can choose to manifest fear. However, if we choose to work with divine laws of the universe from the paradigm of pure love, life becomes less of a struggle.

The truth is that you are not separate from God/Love/Universe and that you are worthy in every way. You are simply obscured from love based on beliefs that you have formed arising from past conditioning, specific circumstances and childhood. The thing is that whatever has happened to you are opportunities for you to learn about love. You are to come into awareness that your essential nature is love.

Love is an energy. It cannot be truly described. Hence you can only truly know it through the qualities that you have experienced. Love is joy in springtime, peace in a prayer, forgiveness in a smile, kindness in an act and intimacy in your relationship. Love is a feeling that lives in your heart. Love always exists. It is in all of us. However, if you have been living in a toxic environment for a long time, you may not be aware that love is present. As the Course in Miracles says, fear blocks your awareness of the presence of love.

Fear is also an energy. However, it is a creation of your mind. Your ego will try its best to convince you that it is real but fear is really an illusion. In the Bhagavad Gita, it is said, "Fear not. What is not real, never was and never will be. What is real, always was and cannot be destroyed." In other words, only love is real. The Bhagavad Gita is the divine discourse spoken by the Supreme Lord Krishna and is the most popular and well known of all the sacred scriptures from ancient India.

There is so much fear created in our environment that it is no surprise that anyone of us will slip into self-loathing easily. Fear exists in your home, school, office, shopping mall, television programs, cinema halls and just about anywhere. You also use fear as a motivator to get yourself, your spouse or children to do the things you want them to.

Fear is what prevents you from giving fully – first to yourself and also to others. Unwittingly, the inability to experience love unconditionally and unreservedly becomes the story pattern of your life. Your psychological wounds arise from fear. Fear creates the belief that you are separate from Source. Fear creates the lack that you experience in your life.

Through letting go of your attachment that creates the fear, you surrender the story of helplessness, hopelessness and wretchedness. You give up control over wanting things according to your way. You are at peace with yourself. You surrender to the serenity inside and outside of you. Doing so activates a healing force that works through your heart.

Ultimately, Source has the all-power to heal. You nurse compassion for the self by the self, which treats the energetic wound. By surrendering your story, you agree to see things with the eyes of unconditional love. You dissolve the illusion that you have been holding on to. Fear dissipates. Surrender simply means giving up the attachment to your old story. You release yourself from your own prison. You are now free.

Unraveling the Paradox

Self-love can sound odd in the beginning. It is hard to wrap the head around the idea of the self being in love with the self. Conventionally, you know love as the bond that binds a relationship between two people. So it can be difficult to grasp the concept that you need to love you. Also, if the self loves the self, it sounds like narcissism and knowing what it means, you are resistant to the thought of turning narcissistic.

Only when you can envisage that there is the possibly more than one self, then things can become a lot easier to understand. The idea of self-love becomes plausible because there is a Self beyond the personality self. It is the Source/God/I AM/Divine Presence that loves the personality self. When this happens, the false or personality self dissolves. The illusory world based on fear that you have previously been living in falls apart.

Your personality self is derived from having an identity. Your identity includes your name, birth details, unique strengths, qualifications and so on. It is important for you to realize that all that you are cannot be known by simply your identity. Hence, you are more than your unique set of birth information, past experiences, achievement records, all forms of identification and labels. There is a presence that is beyond the personality self and that is more accurately, the real you.

Making the distinction between the personality and the true self may seem odd to you as you have been told to refrain from labeling. However, the idea behind the distinction is for easy understanding. Hence, if a reference to a particular self is used, it is not meant to once again reduce the expansive meaning of that which cannot be described by mere words alone. As such, please read this book from the context that it has been written for the easier understanding of spiritual concepts. Now, allow me to proceed.

Your personality self is ruled by the ego. The ego cannot love. It acts out of fear. It spins a web of untruths that hold you back. You are kept small, defeated and feeling worthless. The personality or ego self is an identity that serves as a learning tool. It is not real, therefore. The false self cannot exist in the radiance of awareness. You dissipate its layered stories by becoming aware of the consciousness that lies beneath.

Start off by being able to see that it is the personality self, with all its imperfections, that needs to be embraced. The personality self is otherwise known as the false self or the ego. The problem is that up till now, you have only known yourself as the personality self.

By this understanding, you make the intent to shift and operate from the paradigm of your true self. When you do so, you will do what is best for your inner being. You inadvertently live into self-love. It becomes experiential. You will eventually experience the following: The true self embraces everything about the false self. Its love is all encompassing. In that encompassing, it brings the false self into unity. The false self cannot exist in the space of unifying love. It loses its separate identity. As a result, you become whole and you become One.

Your internal experiences of a shift into wholeness may not be obvious in the beginning. However, you will soon observe the signs. You are more accepting of the self. You even laugh at the slightest mistake you make. You catch yourself in all your booby traps, thus removing yourself from self-sabotage. The ability to recognize insanity as insanity is the start of your sanity. You have awakened to the fact that your true essence goes beyond your thinking mind.

Self-Love is Being

That you are experiencing separation is an internally-created illusion. It has to be solved from within. Hence, addressing something internal cannot be made simply by external means. You cannot claim to love yourself just because you have gone for a top-to-toe spa treatment or bought the latest state-of-the-art gadget. Making such a claim is to be in self-delusion.

Self-love is about your being. It is more than just doing or having. It is more than the endless preoccupation with self-care therapies and material possessions. Self-love is universal consciousness flowing through you. Your body is the vessel through which divine love flows.

Love is the best anti-aging nourishment that you will ever need. You do not need jars of expensive face cream, a bust job or tons of make-up. Results are guaranteed – love keeps you vibrant. When you are in self-love, you gain a radiant glow. Your previously deadened existence springs back to life. It is like having a complete makeover. The change from loving yourself more deeply is powerful because it is from the inside-out.

How do you know if you are being whole? You know this

through using your positive or negative emotions as a guide. Positive emotions are emotions that cause you to feel uplifted, whereas negative emotions cause you to feel poorly. For instance, joy is a positive emotion while anger is a negative emotion. When you are feeling negative emotions, you are being guided to know that you are not in alignment with your spiritual heart or true self. Negative emotions arise when you are feeling inadequate, unlovable and unworthy. You experience shame, rejection, abandonment, anger and so on. They are emotions that come from fear. You are feeling separated.

You cannot be said to have self-love when you are continually experiencing negative emotions. You are more likely to be in disconnection instead. Negative emotions provide you with necessary feedback. And so you take steps with moving into alignment with better-feeling emotions. When you feel peace, calm, warmth and lightness, you are in harmony with your true self. You are in a state of sublime acceptance, grace and wonder. You are in wholeness.

Releasing The Wounds of Your Inner Child

Your inner child stands at the center of your spiritual heart. The "wounded child" is an archetype that is said to contain damaged or negative emotional patterns of your youth. The wounded child can create much havoc in your current relationships with others, if you have not gotten round to resolving past issues. Every time you get triggered in a presenting situation, you are actually re-experiencing the same wound carried by your inner child.

You are kept living in the past. You keep alive the stories of abandonment, rejection, betrayal, abuse, escape, neglect and lack. Healing the wounded child is to embrace the emotions that have been abandoned previously. Your wounded child wants to stay hurt, angry and vindictive. However, as long as you allow your wounded child to be in the driver's seat, you will not be able to operate without fear. And so, you have been collapsing into the same coping mechanisms that help you deal with the original wound. These coping mechanisms could be belief systems or reactions that cause you to suppress, run away, deny, hide or blame.

To love yourself means disallowing wounds of the past to continue to hurt you. You recognize that you are only hurting yourself by carrying your baggage around. Thus, you express willingness to meet your wounded child. And so you call up the child for the unfinished business of loving, nurturing and embracing him or her. You are open to the flood of grief and you agree to let hurt, disappointment, justified anger and vulnerability run its course. The flood of grief inadvertently collapses the barrier walls to your heart.

In the beginning, you may encounter resistance to giving up your story of hurt, trauma, abandonment, rejection and pain. Having identified with the story for so long, you suspect you will feel lost without one. After all, you need someone or something to take the blame for your current dysfunctional self or life. The ego feels good, when fueled by a sense of righteous anger towards your parents, family or friends. Giving up the story makes it feel powerless.

Learn to recognize the need to meet the archetypal force that has kept you in self-sabotage for years. Your actions have largely been driven by fistfuls of fear. While your wounded child has developed coping mechanisms to help you navigate through the valleys of your growing up years, recognize that they no longer serve you now. Invariably, they have kept you in limited patterns of behavior and thinking, as well as negative emotional knee-jerk reactions.

Your childhood story is essentially a collection of thoughts of the past. You have to realize that you cannot hope to create an empowering life if you do not first release your attachment to an old script. You cannot undo the past but you can choose to live in a more positive way forward. Hence, whatever that has wounded you in the past, come to terms with it. Once completed, you are no longer feeding a "poor me" mentality. Old limiting patterns become unstuck. By listening rather than stifling the voice of dissent, you release your inner child from his or her pain.

Spiritual Teachings on Love and Self-Love

Many spiritual teachers teach on love. Jesus teaches the commandment "love your neighbor as yourself". Krishna teaches about compassion. Mother Mary espouses unconditional love. These are all important lessons to loving yourself.

One of my favorite verses on love comes from the Bible. It covers important aspects about what love involves...

> *"Love is patient; love is kind; love is not envious or boastful or arrogant or rude. It does not insist on its own way; it is not irritable or resentful; it does not rejoice in wrongdoing; but rejoices in the truth. It bears all things, believes all things, hopes all things, endures all things."*
> *(1 Corinthians 13: 4-7)*

In particular, what I enjoy are the self-love teachings that come from the enlightened master, The Buddha. The Buddha teaches about the need to love yourself first before you can truly extend the love to others. He observes, "you can travel around the world to search for someone more lovable than yourself, and yet that person is never to be found." In other words, the search is not external but internal. You first find it from within. Allow me to share more about what I know from Buddha's teachings.

To love the self is to be in continuous connection with your true essence. You learn to accept, appreciate and affirm who you are. Unconditional love, acceptance and compassion are divine qualities of your intrinsic nature. When you connect from the inside, you experience the unfolding of wisdom.

An inability to experience true self-love leads to love as something conditional. You love yourself if and only if you fulfill a certain expectation of the self. Your love for others also becomes conditional. It happens when your mind is clouded by perceptions. Hence, the ability for true knowing of the self and others becomes sadly obscured.

Self-realization is key. This means that you are to awaken into love on an experiential basis. You are to actualize it with your own experiencing. As it has been often pointed out, "the finger pointing to the moon is not the moon". All in, Buddha's teachings involve an existential approach, rather than through fuzzy understanding.

From self-love, you lay the ground for the expression of compassion for others. You tune into the sense of shared humanity. You recognize that others are no different from yourself. Everyone is going through essentially the same pain and sorrow – regardless of the various packagings of external circumstances. You extend to others what you would extend to the self. By opening your heart, you gain a gentle-yet-powerful connection with all others.

Loving the self enhances your ability to send metta,

generating energy that is real, pure and transformative. Many Buddhists practice the sending of metta in their prayers. The Buddha shares insightfully, "Hatred can never be ceased by hatred; it is ceased by love alone."

Metta is the radiation of loving kindness towards all beings. The wish is this: *may all beings be well and happy.* True metta is a warm feeling of generosity, compassion, abundance and love that extends beyond all human-imposed boundaries (such as political, racial, social and gender barriers and the divide between human and all others). Metta meditation can supposedly lead one to a state of liberation and freedom.

Love is a practice. The more you practice, the greater your ability to love and be compassionate. It usually starts off as hard work. You have habitual patterns that need to be corrected. You may have already accumulated 1001 reasons why you do not deserve to love yourself. The good news is that it is possible to change what you think and feel. And soon, not just a practice, you lived into love. Ultimately, loving yourself becomes a natural process.

Love is the key to happiness. If you want more happiness, start with practicing having more love for yourself. Then, spread it. Buddha encourages you to share your light, "Thousands of candles can be lit from a single candle, and the life of the candle will not be shortened. Happiness never decreases by being shared."

Story: Wise Woman's Riches

The following is a story written by an unknown author. There once lived a wise woman. She was walking through the forest when she found a stone in a stream. Its brilliance caught her eye. Realizing that it must be precious, she placed it in her bag.

The next day, the wise woman met another traveler who was hungry. He begged her for some food. And so, she opened her bag to share her bread. Just as she was opening her bag, the hungry traveler caught sight of the precious stone. He decided that he wanted the stone for himself and asked the woman to give it to him. She did so without hesitation.

The traveler left, rejoicing in his good fortune. He knew the stone was worth enough to give him security for a lifetime. He was finally rich!

However, a few days later, the traveler went looking for the wise woman. He wanted to return the precious stone to her. He found her eventually. She was sharing her food with another beggar.

"I've been thinking," the traveler said. "I know how valuable this stone is, but I give it back in the hope that you can give me something even more precious."

"Give me what you have within you that enabled you to give me this stone."

CHAPTER SEVEN:
KEYS TO SELF-LOVE

"Appreciation and self-love are the most important tools that you could ever nurture. Appreciation of others, and the appreciation of yourself is the closest vibrational match to your Source Energy of anything that we've ever witnessed anywhere in the Universe."
~Abraham Hicks

Journey Into Self-Love

It is an on-going journey. On some days, it can seem awful. The same debilitating stories come back. You relapse into habitual patterns of harmful thinking, self-bashing and destructive words. Memories of the past flood back to remind you about your old unloving self. During such times, you can be tempted to feel as if all the good that you have tried to do for yourself, has not bore fruit.

What does help is maintaining a state of awareness. Remember that the best opportunity for self-love is when there is most pain. Your aim of it all is to find a way out of the darkness. So, have some faith. Trust that there is light at the end of tunnel. It may mean having to trudge in the dark for some time before reaching an open field of pure light. Hence, do not give up just yet.

Invariably, you will find that the more open you become to yourself, the greater your ability to live into self-love. True inner alchemy holds transformational energy. You are led to unearthing the secrets that have kept you in self-sabotage. Healing takes place when you repair your emotional wounds at the heart no matter how many times or how often it takes. You are continually at your own service.

To love is a decision that you have to make. Love does not happen without you making a conscious decision. Thus, make a stand when it comes to love. When you operate from the space of loving consciousness, you become less vulnerable to the storms in life. As a result, you rest on a foundation that is enduring.

A shift towards love probably shows up gradually in the skip of your walk, the radiance in your smile, the generosity of your spirit, the creativity that you put into your work and the care that you put into your actions. More obvious is the discovery that things are a lot smoother, that you are less prone to negative reactions, and that more and more opportunities are coming by. You find yourself becoming more open to life in its beauty, wonder and mystery.

And so, you become aware that something inside you has changed. You feel, act and believe differently. You are better able to derive greater meaning from a single event. What you used to perceive as a dull moment is now a multidimensional experience of color, brightness and vibrancy. As don Miguel Ruiz in his best-selling book, The Mastery of Love, says, "If you have the eyes of love, you just see love wherever you go."

After you have made the decision, there are a number of things you can do to love yourself. This chapter offers a brief description of keys that I have used personally myself to unlocking the secrets to self-love, in addition to undertaking self-care activities. Self-care activities usually involve the body such as exercising, eating healthily, taking walks in nature and having adequate sleep. They have already been described earlier on.

The ones covered in this chapter are as follows:

- Turn the Self-Talk Inwards
- Recognize Spiritual Lessons From Core Beliefs
- From the Lens of Love
- Flip from Positive to Negative Self-Talk.
- Treat Yourself as a Best Friend.
- Visioning Your Future Self.
- Apply Emotional Freedom Technique
- Practice Mindful Meditation
- Journaling

Self-Love Key: Turn the Self-Talk Inwards

When you examine your inner chatter, you are likely to observe that much of it is also laced with blame, judgment and anger at others. In fact, you may believe that it is more about others than yourself. It appears to be true at first. The trigger usually arises from a loved one, family member or friend. You perceive that someone else is responsible for your pain.

What you may not realize is that you are actually the one hurting yourself. And when you inflict pain inwards, it becomes difficult to love yourself. Hence, to gain realization, turn inwards. Turning inwards involves self-examination.

Note that most therapy work requires you to self-investigate. In fact, a look inwards is necessary for therapy to be effective. During therapy sessions, you will discover that much of your unhappiness arises from your own doing. Anger directed at someone else is a mirror of anger directed inwards.

If a stranger calls you a "pig" and you tell yourself "he just called me a pig" in utter anger and disbelief, you will also have called yourself a pig in your mind. If you keep replaying the "he just called me a pig", you will also have called yourself a pig one hundred more times than the stranger.

In one such session, Jason confided about feeling lousy when he went through a performance appraisal with his boss. His boss did not use the word "stupid" but Jason later realized, upon turning his self-talk inwards, that he had been calling himself "stupid" repeatedly. When we looked at his childhood messages, Jason recalled that his parents implied that he was slow when he was young. While he no longer blames them, he has not found it easy to rid of the label "stupid" that has been stuck in his mind. It has haunted him for a very long time.

If you judge your child to be "a failure", can it be that you believe yourself to be "a failure" for producing "a failure" as a child? If you judge your husband to be "a useless bum", can it be that you are also saying that you are "useless" for sticking it out with a loser? Recognize that you can make the choice to leave a "useless bum" in any moment but you have not.

Linda once got into a conflict situation with her girlfriend, Kristina. Over the course of three weeks, she could not stop judging her. Linda was going on and on with "Kristina did not do this", "Kristina did that" and "I cannot believe that Kristina is like that to me" in her mind. Consumed by righteous anger, Linda felt wronged and how unfair things were. She also started comparing on who contributed more to the friendship. She began to keep score.

Soon, Linda's mind went on an overdrive. If Kristina was "wrong", then she had to be "right". Once activated, her mind pored through past archives to gather evidence that she was "right" in her judgment about Kristina. Linda started recalling all the instances, which she had previously overlooked as small matters. Suddenly what used to be insignificant were now matters of importance. They formed irrefutable proof of what a poor friend Kristina was making.

Still, finding all that proof did not make Linda any happier. Enough, she finally declared, after one particular emotional roller coaster ride. Not enjoying the turbulence, she decided that she did not want to hurt herself any longer. Linda acknowledged that she was in pain.

Having treasured the friendship previously, the breakdown was making her extremely sad. Linda eventually turned the self-talk inwards and recognized the patterns of rejection, blame and deprecation. She realized that not only had she been criticizing Kristina, she was also beating herself up in the process. Linda was also applying the same mental judgments on herself.

I pointed out to Linda that in order to be free, she needed to stop judging. While it might seem that she was being nice not to judge Kristina anymore, she was actually being kind to herself. Ironically, Linda was being given lessons on self-love. After some time, Linda was able to practice enough self-forgiveness. She was also better able to see things from Kristina's perspective. Eventually, her friendship with Kristina mended.

Linda's case is not unique. Everything and everyone is teaching us all the time. Where you feel the most intense irritations are the areas where you can possibly derive important life lessons. In fact, your enemies are your greatest teachers. They are great at pushing your buttons, rocking your boat or rattling your cage. You can cry foul, stomp your feet or curse at them repeatedly. Still, there is no denying the wonderful work that they do. They highlight the areas where you can evolve the most.

If you are in a relationship that is in trouble right now, you may have been tempted to think of it as a bad mistake. You curse at yourself for being blind in not picking up the signs. You wonder why you have not managed to spot the trait in your partner that has also similarly driven you away from your parents. Well, there is no mistake. You have been given the opportunity to find yourself again, through a reenactment of a similar situation.

It takes courage to face your denials, shame, rejection, wounds, flaws, imperfections or anything that makes you feel vulnerable. Through experiencing separation from others, you learn about separation from your true self. In reality, it is the illusion of separation that has caused you to suffer much inner conflict. Since separation is created from psychological fear, it is not real. Your negative emotions let you know that you are out-of-alignment. Through a process of shifting towards better feelings, you find a way out of your mental traps.

Oddly enough, through inner awareness, you also get a glimpse into the true nature of all relationships; including the war that you are currently fighting against your spouse, parent or friend. You start to develop empathy. You are now able to put yourself in their shoes and come in touch with their deepest suffering.

And so, you start to drop what is no longer important. You become more appreciative of the good that is already happening in your life. Meaning becomes more alive inside you. You will ultimately discover that you hold the key to your own happiness. And the key to unlock it is through self-love. By deciding that you wish to be happy, it would not do to put yourself in any more unnecessary pain. You have got a choice. And you make the choice to be free.

Spiritual transcendence happens when you are able to turn the problem inwards. You use your mind as the laboratory, where you investigate your self-talk. Your investigations lead you to accessing deeper truths about yourself. While it may involve buckets and buckets of tears, you will eventually discover the pricelessness of self-knowledge. Your tears wash away the pains of your yesterdays. You have freed your wounded child from being held captive within the deep caverns of your soul.

Self-Love Key: Recognize Spiritual Lessons From Core Beliefs

A close look into your internal dialogue can be very revealing. You peel through the layers in order to arrive at your core beliefs. It boils down to three that are behind your negative self-talk regarding loving yourself:

- I don't love myself because I am not lovable.
- I don't love myself because I am not good enough.
- I don't love myself because I am not worthy or deserving.

The beliefs are pretty much ingrained, thus you identify yourself by them. You believe them to be real. Where they are not as easily detectable, they probably lie in your subconscious underneath the multitude layers of your self-talk. Limiting core beliefs can cause you to be in self-sabotage continually for years.

Your spiritual lessons are often related to these core beliefs. The more you believe yourself as undeserving, the more certain you will become over time about your unworthiness. Your capacity to receive love is limited to the amount of love that you can give to yourself. Because the core beliefs are not easily eliminated, it would appear that these beliefs form lifelong lessons.

Self-love starvers or those with tremendous difficulties with loving themselves are more likely to have beliefs that are more deeply rooted. Seldom feeling enough, they go around looking for love. Driven to desperation, they often settle for options that cause them to experience more pain than love. Invariably, they become more cynical about life. Their cynicism is a mirror of inherently feeling lousy from the inside. Every little thing sets them off on a whole plethora of negative emotions.

Triggers that set these beliefs off can be found in various situations that present themselves. Presenting issues can be anything that causes you an emotional disruption. Hence, what you do is to trace each presenting issue or self-talk pattern and see if it leads you to the few or one common root belief. You will invariably find that many of your situations do. You may even be shocked that everything that is happening to your life right now is related to your core beliefs.

Examples of triggers include:

"I am not lovable because I am born imperfect.
"I am not lovable because no one likes me."
"I am not lovable because I am not good enough."
"I am not lovable because my mummy does not spend enough time with me."
"I am not lovable because I have got no friends."
"I am not lovable because I am not special."
"I am not lovable because my parents abandon me."
"I am not lovable because I have been physically abused."
"I am not lovable because I have sinned."
"I am not lovable because my spouse left me for someone else."
"I am not lovable because I have got big feet."
"I am not lovable because I have got small boobs."

"I am not good enough to write a book."
"I am not good enough to be a parent."
"I am not good enough to make more money."
"I am not good enough to be an inspiring role model."
"I am not good enough to do healing work."
"I am not good enough to be psychic."
"I am not good enough because I am not capable enough."

"I am not good enough because I am not successful."
"I am not good enough because I am born imperfect."
"I am not good enough because I do not have qualifications."
"I am not good enough because I am being undermined."
"I am not good enough because I am feeling small."
"I am not good enough because I am less intelligent."
"I am not good enough because I am not as good as him or her."
"I am not good enough because I get a smaller scoop of ice cream."
"I am not good enough because I am not lovable."

"I am not deserving of a healthy relationship."
"I am not deserving of success."
"I am not deserving of love."
"I am not deserving of more attention from my spouse."
"I am not deserving of good health."
"I am not deserving of kindness."
"I am not deserving of a good time."
"I am not worthy of my mother's love."
"I am not worthy of receiving this award."
"I am not worthy of good fortune."
"I am not worthy of the compliment that I have just received."

The only difference between all the above sentences lies in the tail end. The tail ends are the triggers or presenting situations. You are likely to find yourself alternating between the sentences in your self-talk as you go about your day; from home, to the school or office and in social settings.

Because of the subtle nuance between them, the phrases of "I am not lovable", "I am not good enough" and "I am not deserving" can seemingly overlap each other. In some situations, only one phrase applies; yet in others, all can apply. In cases where a person feels loved but still suffers from inadequate self-love, it is less of an issue of being unlovable than a case of "I am not good enough" or "I am undeserving".

Take, for instance, my friend, Adeline. She has a doting father who calls her his "darling princess". He has been placing a lot of hopes on her, as she is an only child. Adeline's father is a top lawyer who works long hours. He was hardly ever around when she was growing up. However, he tried to make it up to her by buying her expensive gifts whenever he came home from an overseas business trip.

Suffering from chronic depression, Adeline's mother was mostly absent too. It was a rather lonely childhood for Adeline, as there was little communication or bonding time. Although she is now an adult, Adeline finds that she faces tremendous challenges from living in the shadow of poor self-esteem. In her mind, it is clear that she is lovable but simply "not good enough" or worthy. She feels as if she can never measure up or can ever be good enough for her father to pay some attention to her.

Awareness helps, obviously. First, you clear stuck energies that keep you living in the past. You heal your wounded child. Second, you also become alert to yourself. You catch yourself when a new situation triggers the same belief again. You recognize your own traps and avoid falling into the same emotional patterns of feeling abandoned, rejected, unaccepted, insignificant and betrayed. Once again, Ralph Waldo Emerson has got excellent advice for us, "Let me never fall into the vulgar mistake of dreaming that I am persecuted whenever I am contradicted. "

With increasing awareness, you are able to stand apart from your old self. You realize that you are not the story that you have been telling yourself. Getting into a space of stillness helps. From stillness, you tune into a consciousness that is beyond thought. You realize that you are innately lovable because pure love is your basic essence. You are also worthy regardless of any presenting situation that tries to trick you into believing otherwise. Awakened from your illusion, you live life with greater clarity. You are finally deeply aware that you are enough and that you are love.

Self-Love Key: Operate From the Perspective of Love

To operate from a loving perspective requires you to make a clear intent to shift away from ego consciousness. You refuse to dwell in fear, anger or resentment. In other words, you make the conscious choice to perceive things from the lens of love. You choose to reframe your perception to the way that best supports yourself and in the highest good of all concerned. For making belief changes at the identity level, the most powerful way is to align with your true self.

Your ego or identity is subject to constant change. When you are identified with the ego, your personality state is affected by changing emotions, beliefs and awareness. The changes are triggered by your life experiences. Hence, ego consciousness is not absolute. However, the presence that is beneath the personality is eternal, infinite and never-changing. It is of divine love and hence, is all-inclusive.

Consider putting yourself in the position of your true or wise self in order to find a more loving way to respond to life. When you do this often enough, you will ultimately realize that who you are goes beyond a set of fixed ideas, concepts or beliefs. Having a spiritual practice that will lead you to a deep spacing of knowing helps. Ultimately, it does not matter which spiritual or religious practice you choose to apply; since all paths teach you about unconditional love.

For a start, ask yourself the following questions:

How would life look like when you operate from the position of your true or wise self?

What story would your wise or true self tell?

With your new story, could things change for you?

How would your relationships look like?

Here are some reframes that you can use for shifting into alignment with your true self:

- I am essentially not a bad person. I am just a person who has acted unwisely.

- I choose to accept myself regardless of success or failure.

- I do not have to wait till the "perfect moment" to determine whether I am worthy or not.

- I view failures as opportunities for learning and growth.

- I am not a loser just because I have made a mistake.

- It is anybody's guess. My guess is just as good as anyone else's.

- I did the best I could, based on the knowledge and circumstances that were present back then.

- Everyone makes mistakes. I am willing to forgive and move on from here.

- I am perfection even with all my imperfections.

- To be human is to take a risk. Growth can only happen when I am in discomfort.

When you wear the lens of love, everything falls in line. You make choices that will take care of your needs in a holistic way. It may feel weird sounding loving all of a sudden at first but the more you practice, the more you will be able to move into alignment with your true or wise self. Everyone benefits when you operate from a loving perspective.

Self-Love Key: Flip From Negative to Positive Self-Talk

Most certainly, it would help to have a list of daily affirmations that would help you make a positive shift. The affirmations are what you would like to see yourself from the lens of love. Keep a record of the negative self-talk that you have been engaging in. Then, turn it around into a list of positive affirmations.

Self-Rejection	========➔	Self-Acceptance
Self-Blame	========➔	Self-Forgiveness
Self-Deprecation	========➔	Self-Esteem
Self-Criticism	========➔	Self-Compassion
Self-Neglect	========➔	Self-Care
Self-Doubt	========➔	Self-Trust
Self-Pity	========➔	Self-Empowerment

Rules to Apply For Positive Affirmations

Reframe the affirmations in the positive. Affirm what you

want in terms of outcome rather than what you do not. For instance, affirm "I accept myself" rather than "I do not reject myself".

Ban unhelpful words. Avoid using words like "must", "should", "hate" and "can't" from your vocabulary. All of these words are energy depleting words. By banning unhelpful words and language from your internal scripts, your self-talk becomes more positive.

Feel the Emotional Impact. When affirming, feel the emotional impact of your affirmation. When you can actually "feel" your affirmation, not just utter or read them, its impact increases immensely. You connect strongly with your new intention. Strong intention summons powerful thought energy.

Align with your inner truths. You probably would find it hard to believe your positive self-talk wholeheartedly or overnight. So it is crucial that you do not lie to yourself. Simply, state the truth as it-is. Thus, choose affirmations that do not sound too difficult to believe in. For instance, saying "I have every ability to succeed" may be too far a stretch as compared to "I can do this once I really set my mind to." The qualifier "once I really set my mind to" helps to make the affirmation more believable for a start.

Taking Abraham Hick's suggestion on telling better-feeling stories, I have turned positive affirmations into a story script. When I first got started, my ego will be up in arms about what I was going to do for a personal growth makeover. It did not like to have its voice over-written. Having a script helps to break down any resistance to making immediate changes. It serves as a great way to negotiate with the ego in a gradual fashion. You lead yourself through a process of alignment.

Below is a script that I have used for myself. You can use it as an example to write your own.

My Positive Self-Talk Script

I love myself. I am unique. There is no one else quite like me. There is no one else with the same gifts, talents, experiences, strengths or appearance. Then again, there are things about me that are imperfect or flawed. However, I choose to accept all of me completely, unconditionally and absolutely.

I fully embrace the emotions that arise whenever I have thoughts like "I am unlovable", "I am not good enough" and "I am not worthy". Nonetheless, a part of me also observes that these labels put me in a state of contraction. I become aware of this part of me that observes. And I choose to rest my attention on this knowing part of me. I recognize that whenever I lean towards this wise part of me, I feel better immediately.

Love is a choice. And, I choose love. As the author to my own life script, I now make the choice to rewrite it to one that is positive, uplifting and helpful for my well-being. While others had helped me write my inner script for years, I am taking back ownership. I now affirm: I am lovable, loving and loved.

I understand that my old inner script has been pretty much of the past. I accept that it is a product of childhood conditioning, old habits and limited thought patterns. Thus, I commit myself to examining the beliefs that may have served me in the past but are no longer useful for my present and the future.

I make the intention to release myself from the past. What is past is past. I release any attachment to my old script. Where I have made any mistakes, I forgive myself and I forgive all those who have contributed to the situation. I choose to heal right here, right now. My past offers me valuable learning lessons. I learn from them, so that I am able to move forward. I find that the more I apply these lessons positively, the closer I will align with the outcome I desire.

I also intend to connect with love from my heart. I see myself as someone who is connected, whole, confident, abundant, fulfilled, secure and peaceful. I honor my dreams. I am abundant, with ample resources and close access to my spiritual team. It may take a while before the self-loving me manifests but I understand that as long as I continue to affirm my new story, I am on track in manifesting the picture I hold in my mind.

Regardless, I am aware that I am more than my identity. Who I am goes beyond my thoughts, emotions and beliefs. Aligning body, heart, mind and spirit, I am divine presence; eternal, infinite and beautiful. Love is my basic nature. Love shines from my soul through my being. I am Love in eternity.

Self-Love Key: Treat Yourself Like A Best Friend

If thinking in spiritual terms seems uncomfortable for you as a start, another practical way to self-love is to treat yourself like a best friend. As in a friendship, it is important to engage in healthy, honest and open communication. You use language that is positive, uplifting and engaging. With the self, it involves being authentic. You are patient, open and feel safe to explore your discomforts. To be a true friend, you

cultivate the following ingredients:
- Authenticity
- Compassion
- Support
- Acceptance
- Responsibility
- Respect

You show the same level of genuine care you would give to a friend, if not more. You look deeply into yourself and understand your own sufferings. You give yourself the space to grow, make mistakes and learn from them. It is how you show compassion.

You are also willing to express yourself creatively. You do not censure, rebuke, judge or criticize. You also refrain from overreacting to problems, perceiving signs of rejection when none existed and also distrusting your inner guidance.

Feeling comfortable is very important. So being able to relax and being at ease is essential. You learn how to be with the self, even when there is no one else around. And you feel comfortable being in silence. You are not feeling panicky, restless or bored in your own company. You are able to sit still, fully present to yourself.

Best of all, you can even laugh at yourself. Laughing is a sign of inner harmony. And so, you laugh at your silly obsessions, nutty behavior and crazy phobias. You are not laughing in deprecation but with good humor. You can even laugh at yourself in the company of your family and friends. There is enough self-acceptance to know that it is okay for others to join in the laughter. You can do this because you are already best friends with yourself.

Self-Love Key: Have A Vision of Your Authentic Self

When you look at yourself in the mirror, are you focusing on the reflection of your imperfections or do you see yourself wholly in a reflection with the most radiant smile, is genuinely happy and exuding calmness? Famous actress, Drew Barrymore, once said, "I used to look in the mirror and feel shame, I look in the mirror now and absolutely love myself."

Have a vision of what you would like to see in the mirror a few months from now. Holding on to a vision keeps your dreams alive for you. You find yourself less likely to get distracted or lose the commitment to self. Real change takes place when you do not waiver.

Hence, see if you can paint the following vision. As you shift towards greater self-love, you begin to see a more attractive picture of yourself in the mirror. It is the same reflection that others are looking at. You no longer hide behind the façade of a false self. You are your authentic self. Others love and accept you for who you are. You are whole. There is no more inner conflict because you are expressing the self you are inside.

Through self-love, you shift the center of power to your being; rather than placing it somewhere else. It is a position of strength. You know that you will always be there for yourself. Even when times are bad, you do not abandon the self. Under no circumstances do you deny your true feelings, hopes and dreams.

Your self-talk becomes positive, encouraging and uplifting. Ultimately, you will discover that what you say about and others carry the same resonance too. You transform from a person who is seeped in negativity to someone who is joyous, generous and passionate. You become a beacon of love.

Love is energy. When you love yourself truly, the energy extends into divine love for all. Love is the golden thread that binds everyone and everything in the universe. Your relationships with others create a beautiful weave. It is a weave that includes the sky, the earth, the sun, the stars and the moon. It is a weave created meaningfully with each moment well lived. Together, all contributes to a brilliant tapestry.

I could sense Paul's changing demeanor during a visioning exercise that I facilitated. His eyes were closed. But he was far from being asleep. Paul was actively picturing how he would like to see himself one year down the road. His vision was someone who would be enjoying all the benefits that come with a greater sense of self-love and esteem. Paul spoke with growing conviction. His face became flushed and he waved his hands with excitement, as he spoke. I noticed a glistening sparkle when he finally opened his eyes.

Self-Love Key: Apply Emotional Freedom Technique

Emotional Freedom Technique or EFT is a method that involves tapping on specific meridian points on your face and body to neutralize negative emotions. It is like applying acupuncture without the needles, but just using your fingers to tap. EFT works well for a variety of situations, including issues on low self-love.

EFT is a method developed by Gary Craig. It involves the verbalizing of a positive healing statement. When your energy system is balanced, the body's natural healing abilities are restored. The healing statement is that "even though I feel or believe (negative emotion or limiting belief),

I deeply and completely love and accept myself." With a healing statement like this, it is easy to see why EFT is excellent for self-acceptance and compassion.

The sentence introduces equanimity. This means that you embrace your negative emotions, acknowledging that they are there but that it is okay to have them. You give yourself the permission to have them in your experience. When you allow yourself to feel your aversions completely, they miraculously dissolve.

There are little or no negative side effects reported since EFT does not involve any invasive surgical procedures, pills or pushing and pulling on the body. I have gained tremendously from using this method and have used it on clients, friends and family as well. While results can vary, there have been many cases of instantaneous release of negative emotions. For more information on this technique, please check out the website http://www.eftuniverse.com.

Self-Love Key: Practice Mindfulness Meditation

Realize that either extremes of self-deprecation or narcissism is not healthy. On the other hand, balanced awareness is important. The practice that comes to mind is one of equanimity. Equanimity can be cultivated through mindfulness meditation.

Indeed, it is very difficult to stop your inner critic from talking. Buddhists call it the monkey mind – the non-stop chatter as you jump from one thought to the next. Practicing mindfulness can help slow down the monkey mind. Mindfulness is observing what it says but not getting caught in the emotional content. It involves present moment awareness.

You are like a witness, a silent observer. Without any reaction, you are simply observing your thoughts. Thus, you practice not-attachment to your thoughts or thinking process. You do not feed your negative emotions. You are also not about to change or fix anything. Gradually, your conscious detachment dissolves the pain from your self-talk that you have been holding on to.

Equanimity is a state of mental or emotional stability or composure arising from a deep awareness and acceptance of the present moment. You are neither attached nor averse. Cultivating equanimity is far from becoming dull, inactive or indifferent. The Buddha described a mind filled with equanimity as "abundant, exalted, immeasurable, without hostility and without ill-will." According to Christian philosophy, equanimity is considered essential for carrying out the theological values of gentleness, contentment, temperance and charity.

Start off by learning how to practice mindfulness in a meditative setting. Meditating in a peaceful environment helps especially if you are a beginner. You set aside time for dedicated practice. Ultimately, the idea is to be able to apply mindful awareness throughout the day. You bring an awakened state of consciousness to your everyday life. When you do so, you find yourself less likely to react emotionally to triggering situations. You are more peaceful, calm and centered.

Mindfulness practice offers many benefits. Neuro-imaging studies have shown that when people consider their problems mindfully, they use additional brain circuits beyond those that simply involve problem solving. Many randomized-controlled trials have also already proven that mindfulness can be effective in combating depression, insomnia, anxiety disorders, and social phobias. In fact, there have been studies that show mindfulness-based therapies are as good as antidepressants.

As an observer or witness, you become conscious of the thinking mind. However, as you stay continue to stay present, you also discover a consciousness arising that goes far beyond labels, name-calling and crippling self-talk. Your illusions shatter to reveal the truth. You awaken to the eternal essence of love that has always been there. Life with the magic of grace, peace and joy unfolds moment-to-moment.

Self-Love Key: Journaling

If you have not already started on journaling, I suggest you do. It is probably one of the best-kept secrets for self-love. It is therapy that is low-cost but provides tremendous benefits. You can gain awareness on things about yourself that you have not previously known.

A journal comprises of your thoughts, feelings, observations, insights and analysis. Because it is private, you are free to express without receiving a word of judgment or critic from anyone else. It is a safe outlet especially when you find it hard to reveal your vulnerabilities to anyone. During challenging times, journaling may just be the thing that ploughs you through.

By presenting the opportunity to review your feelings, journaling offers you emotional relief. It is a safe place for you to examine your self-talk. You discover that there can be possibly be more than one perspective in looking at things. Journaling helps you to open up possibilities for thinking, problem-solving and new revelations.

Journaling can also serve as a playground, whereby there is freedom to explore creative ideas before sharing any with someone. It holds your best-kept secrets about your dreams, hopes, visions and wishes. If you find yourself consistently going back to any single one of them, it may be a highlight on what you need to pursue.

The wonderful part about journaling is that there are no rules. You do not have to have excellent English writing skills or dot your "i" as you so wish. There is no need to have it vetted by your teacher. You can write bad poetry if you want to. What is great is that you are able to write instinctively. Not holding yourself back, you allow your thoughts and feelings to flow.

Journaling has certainly been an important tool for my self-discovery. I never thought that I would enjoy it so much. While I started off with wanting to find an emotional outlet for myself, I eventually found out that it helped enhance my creativity skills. I have since moved on to doing art journals, as a way to being inspired and reminding myself of all the wonderful miracles in life.

Journaling has a way of leading me back to my center. It helps me see how unique I am. It helps me appreciate the way I am. Journaling allows me to be fully present to my inner world and assists me with channeling insights in a creative manner. I turn to journaling whenever I am feeling blue. A treasure of gems, my journal has been a constant source of inspiration for me.

Self-Love Key: Surround Yourself With Supportive Family and Friends

Admittedly, it can be a challenge trying to love yourself if you live in a toxic environment of people who keep putting you down. These people are likely to have more issues on self-love themselves relatively. Thus, you find it hard to stay positive. Their verbal abuse wears you down. They can be people in the office, friends or even family members.

Toxic people are either skilled in poking holes or dampening your aura. You experience a sense of dread, misery, illness and nervous energy, whenever you have to be near people with toxic energy. You feel drained energetically after spending a mere 10 minutes with them. Eventually, you find yourself having to make excuses for not showing up in meetings or for your disappearance.

As someone who has low self-love, it is also possible that you let toxic people take away your individual rights to choice. Lacking in confidence, you are not able to put your foot down. Unconsciously, you allow your happiness be dictated by their irrational fears. If your toxic relationship is in a romantic or family situation, you are likely to experience trauma and pain. You will find it hard to walk away immediately if there are blood or close ties involved.

Edward is 45 years old but who still suffers from a torrent of emotional abuse whenever he visits his mother. Till today, his mother tells him, "you will never succeed", "you are so useless" and "you are born with bad karma". Edward had to move out from his family home years ago as he could not withstand the pain and suffering from his mother's toxic energy. Instead of welcoming him, his mother continues to berate him as she has always done during his weekly visits.

In a jab of low confidence, which happens often enough, Edward would wonder if what his mother says is true. Edward has suffered tremendously as a result of his low self-love and esteem. He has contemplated suicide several times, could not sustain relationships and found it difficult to thrive well in his job.

Hence, to help yourself be more self-loving, be more selective about the people you spend time with. Surround yourself with people who are loving, positive or those who use uplifting words and behavior. Choose those who are inspiring, motivational, embody a sense of inner calm, like-minded, lifelong learners and keen on spiritual development. If you are not able to get warmth and support from family members, consider looking elsewhere. Join interest groups or form a supportive group yourself.

Perhaps the best that you can do is to create a sacred circle. As you already know, the circle is a shape that has no sides. Hence, it is symbolic of the sharing of hearts in an open, honest and trusting platform. We borrow the idea from Alcoholics Anonymous where addicts have managed to free themselves from dependency by being part of a group where each member has felt safe to share, without judgment.

In a sacred circle, you are given the space to speak freely the emotions that have been repressed for years. The moment that you express your truth, you would have unblocked your heart. While loving yourself still requires your inner participation, you have just made your journey less of a challenge by having a group of supportive friends forged through mutual bonding.

CHAPTER EIGHT:
HEART OF LIVING WITH
SELF-LOVE

*"To love oneself is the beginning
of a lifelong romance".
- Oscar Wilde (1854-1900)*

Love Is All Around

Just imagine experiencing love all around. You can see it, feel it and sense it. It is in the kaleidoscope of the morning dewdrops, the melodious chorus of the birds, the blossoming smiles of a pretty daisy, the after-glow of the evening sun, the shimmer across the moonlit lake and the vastness of the cosmic night sky. Each aspect of love expressed in its glorious magnificence is being weaved to form a beautiful ever-changing canvas. It is a tapestry of total perfection in every single moment.

Not only is love experienced in the surroundings of nature, you also get to enjoy its quintessential qualities in your everyday relationships. Love is comfort in a bear hug, connection in a shared teacup, kindness in a neighborly act, grace in a genuine smile and wisdom in a helpful advice. Whether as a giver or a receiver of love, you are inspired, renewed, and healed. There is meaning to be discovered, with the unfolding of time. Each moment touched by love is forever transformed in its experiencing.

From the space of love, you experience a consciousness that is deep, fulfilling and infinite. You feel it from deep down the center of your heart. It is a consciousness that extends beyond the reaches of time, space and matter. It is beyond anything conceivable. No words can describe your experience simply. Delving in, you become oneness in the field of eternal bliss. It is the space of nothingness and it is also, the space of everything.

As you read the above paragraphs, you may start to laugh. You are possibly laughing in disbelief. All that has been described can sound like some new age woo-hoo talk that is too surreal to be true. Any magical experience seems far off from where you are currently. You find it hard to imagine any new possibility. After all, you have lived with a closed heart for a very long time. You face the fear of coming into contact with the rawness of life. Thus, your preference is to shield yourself even if it means locking your own heart.

Well, if you have not experienced anything so beautiful, know that it is just as available to you as it is to anyone else. Most certainly, I do not think a magical experience of any sort is exclusive. Hence, it is not reserved just for those who have psychic powers or superhuman abilities. Anyone with the clear intent to practicing self-love will be led to the same loving space.

I cannot profess to have reached a state of enlightenment but I have my glimpses to know that there is something that is far more than our everyday consciousness. Self-love is pretty much a spiritual process, offering pure beauty in its most magnificent moments. What is true is that when I said yes to self-love, I encountered miracles. I began to see meaning in everything that unfolded before me. I have not felt this much joy. I also found that there is no shortage when it comes to love. Any lack is only experienced with a heart that is not completely open.

Miracles happen when you see through the lens of love. As Zen Buddhist Master, Thich Nhan Hanh, says "People usually consider walking on water or in thin air a miracle. But I think the real miracle is not to walk either on water or in thin air, but to walk on earth. Every day we are engaged in a miracle which we don't even recognize: a blue sky, white clouds, green leaves, the black, curious eyes of a child -- our own two eyes. All is a miracle." To experience miracles fully requires you to connect with your heart. You need to first open it to receive the miracles.

Love is everywhere. Water too. As with our bodies, about

70% of Earth is also covered with water. Water when stagnant becomes dirty, murky and toxic. On the other hand, water needs to flow through the rivers, lakes and oceans for it to be fresh, renewing and revitalizing. Water transports energy. And water can transport love. While it is true that we cannot do without water, we can also best survive with water that is clean and free-flowing. We thrive well with water that is energized with the power of love.

Dr Masaru Emoto is a Japanese researcher who believes that water has memory and can contain messages. His work demonstrates how consciousness can impact the molecular structure of water. To show the effects, he takes photographs of the crystals formed after freezing and exposing water to specific words, prayers, music and intentions. In his groundbreaking best-selling book, "The Hidden Messages of Water", Dr Emoto has found that that the words "love and gratitude" created the most beautiful hexagonal structure with intricate branches, while toxic words created the most distorted and disturbing structures.

Since our bodies are comprised of 70% water, it implies that we can enjoy positive internal changes when we say positive things to ourselves. Based on his findings, it would appear that "love and gratitude" is the most powerful healing message as compared to the rest. In his second book, "The True Power of Water", Dr Emoto also demonstrated the effects of using antonyms from at first using negative words with the same sample of water. There were marked changes. He consistently found that water responded in beautiful crystals to words like "happiness", "angel" and "peace" and in broken and unbalanced crystals to words like "unhappiness", "devil" and "war" respectively.

This brings to mind the suggestion on flipping our negative self-talk patterns into their exact opposites. It will be great to have Dr Emoto conduct experiments measuring the effect from self-hatred to self-love or specially using the words of self-rejection, self-blame, self-deprecation, self-criticism, self-neglect, self-denial, self-doubt and self-pity to their antonyms of self-acceptance, self-forgiveness, self-esteem, self-compassion, self-care, self-nurture, self-trust and self-empowerment. While a good guess on what the results will be like can already be made, it will also be interesting to see the pictures of the water crystals formed after being exposed to phrases like "I love myself", "I accept myself" and "I am enough".

Whole-hearted Living

Self-love is wholehearted living that involves the consideration of holistic balance. Integrating towards wholeness, you incorporate all aspects of mind, body and spirit. You cannot claim to be in wellness if you ignore or sacrifice one or more aspects for another.

More often than not, we make decisions that ignore our souls. We prefer to rely only on our five senses. We prefer not to know what is happening at the spiritual level, because we fear that it would get in the way of pursuing our materialistic dreams. We sense a potential conflict. Furthermore, should we involve our spirit, it will mean having to allocate time to get to know ourselves.

However, there is no other way. Self-discovery is an important part to the process of integrating into wholeness. When you are feeling whole, you know: *I am enough*. In wholeness, there is no lack. You also do not experience any disconnection or separation from Source. Wholeness is fulfilled by pure love coming from within. It is love that flows endlessly. Conversely, wholeness cannot be fulfilled by material possessions or outward sources of gratification. If you seek externally, you will never be satisfied for long. You will always feel as if a vital ingredient of yourself is missing.

The vision of wholeness turns to reality, so long as you hold on to it. Wholeness is abundance. You enjoy every aspect of wellness. You will never be short because you are certain that you are enough. Fullness from the level of being leads to fullness at the level of having. Because you believe that you are enough in every sense of the word, your reality shifts to affirm its truth. You will ultimately discover how powerful you are as a co-creator of the world around you.

The Gift of Presence

Presence is a great gift for cultivating unconditional love and acceptance. Yet, it may be something that you often overlook because you are constantly in a rush. Because there are just too many conflicting demands, you find it hard to slow down. Priorities that are actually important such as spending time with your family get the least attention from you.

I remember a question posed by Ajahn Brahmavamso Mahathera (also known as Ajahn Brahm), abbot of Bodhinyana Monastery in Western Australia, poignantly when I was at his talk some years back. The question was: who do you think the most important person is? Most of us are likely to guess this person to be our spouse, child or parent. Well, the answer is this: the most important person is the one seated next to you at any moment in time.

Hence, this means that when you are in conversation with this friend, your mind is not somewhere else. It also means that when you are in the office, you do not worry about matters at home. And vice versa. You give your friend, spouse, child or who ever you are with, your utmost attention.

To build strong relationships, presence is necessary. It is not enough to be present just in thought. Physical presence counts. Hence, it is both quality and quantity time. The most important moment is the here and now. And to be fully present is to listen with an open heart. You do not allow judgments or criticism to enter while listening. You are patient, kind and understanding.

Presence is obviously needed when it comes to cultivating relationships with others. It is the same with building a relationship with the self. So the questions really are: *Are you present with yourself? Are you present to everything that is about you – your thoughts, emotions, inner dreams and desires?*

Self-love involves the gift of presence. This means that you give yourself balanced attention. You become fully aware of your self-talk. However, you are not caught up in its emotional content. You spend time getting to know the most intimate parts about yourself. However, you do not become overly self-absorbed; thereby losing touch with your physical surroundings. By being fully present, while in sublime silence, you provide the opportunity for deep universal truths to emerge from your soul.

Healthy self-loving should not lead to obsession with the self. Rather than be trapped within the confines of a torturous mental landscape, you are able to maintain presence with the world around you. Inadvertently, when you do so, you connect with the deeper truths of what it means to engage your heart. You love yourself from the essence of who you are. Love heals every cell inside your body gently but surely. There is no stopping this flow. In its abundance, you awaken to the miracle of existence and being in this world.

Manifesting Abundance through Self-Love

Not many of us are aware of the relationship between manifesting abundance and self-love. We are not aware that changing our external reality starts with working on the self. Mostly, we work on trying to fix other people rather than ourselves. We prefer to push blame and we refuse to take personal responsibility. We look outwards rather than inwards for answers to our problems.

Everyday, we would dream about having a life of abundance. However, many of us fall into the trap of believing that more abundance can be found by earning more money. So we work harder. Because we spend our available time in the office chasing datelines, we do not have the luxury of sitting down to have a proper meal with our family and friends. Unfortunately, all that chasing puts us in a constant struggle.

Thus, we find ourselves constantly complaining. We feel unwell. There is no space to just be. We are caught too much in the doing in our chase for the "having". However, instead of exuding the vibration of "having", we exude "not having". Mostly, we are unhappy because we have not "arrived" at our desired goal. Since like attracts like according to the Law of Attraction, an energetic resonance of "not having" attracts more of "not having".

What you need to realize is that the vibration of abundance is love. Love is power. Love has the ability to create. It creates miracles. It creates everything that you see around you. There is only one way to live your life, if you ever want to be abundant. And it is to love yourself. I cannot imagine anyone as being truly abundant if he or she is in self-hatred or starving of love.

Hence, if you want to attract wonderful relationships, open your heart to receive. Self-love is where you need to start. By being nourished from within, you naturally exude a healthy radiance. You view the world with a loving perspective and you express love in everything that you do. Love is your ultimate truth. Loving yourself allows your soul to shine through. It is how you open the door for divine grace to enter into your life.

Most certainly, expanding your heart space brings about many benefits:

First, your heart is the spiritual vessel through which love pours. By opening your heart space, you allow yourself to receive. You increase the bounty. You can only give what your heart holds. You are able to receive and give love in plentiful supply. If it is not clear enough, you need to come from a place of fullness in order to manifest a life in abundance. You cannot come from a place of starvation, diet or limitation. The more love calories you have, the better.

Second, your heart holds the seat to a lion's courage. Courage is needed to explore the darkest chamber of your childhood secrets. To begin with, the heart is a repository of stories waiting to unfold. It leads to the locked chambers of your secrets. Your participation is required in that you need to turn the lock and allow healing energies to pass through. Love then weaves its way through your heart and leads you to freedom.

Third, your heart holds the secrets to your deepest desires as well. By connecting with your heart, you awaken your authentic dreams. At the juncture where passion meets purpose, you bring forward these dreams into manifestation.

Fourth, opening your heart allows you to access your spiritual birthright. It can be difficult connecting with spirit if you are blocked in the fourth chakra. Opening your heart allows spiritual blessings to enter. Since love is the most powerful energy, you are able to harness it fully to lead an abundant life.

Love is your soul magnet. Love in the soul attracts more love. You are a magnet of spiritual positive energy. Others become drawn to you. They like feeling uplifted. Your positive energy rubs off on them. Because you feel worthy, attracting positive outcomes also becomes easy. Life flows smoothly, as a result.

Abundance is the capacity to live fully. Contentment is the soil for abundance. It allows abundance to flourish in the garden of your soul. Contentment can never be derived from external gratification alone. True contentment needs to start from a place of self-acceptance. It is about loving yourself unconditionally. When you vibrate "I am enough", you will tend to attract more of the energetic resonance of "I am enough" in its various manifestations.

Obviously, it is important to participate in life fully. It is like playing a game. Be it tennis, volleyball, monopoly or chess, you hope to come out strong on the winning end. The game of life is the game of love. Love is the divine plan. The plan unfolds through you. To play well, absolute presence is necessary. And hence, you commit spirit to your everyday existence. It means that you live with love from your heart fully.

Heart of Self-Love

> *"Love is what we were born with. Fear is what we have learned here. The spiritual journey is the relinquishment – or unlearning – of fear and the acceptance of love back into our hearts. Love is...our ultimate reality and our purpose on earth. To be consciously aware of it, to experience love in ourselves and others, is the meaning of life."*
> *– Marianne Williamson*

You come full circle in your journey from within. As soon as you are born, you start to learn about fear. Fear is created because you believe that you cannot get what you want. Your disconnection arises out of separation. So long as you are feeling separated, you have a self-love issue. Love is blocked in its flow when you place obstacles such as judgment, pain and misery in its way. Inadvertently, you are obscured from experiencing your true nature.

Starving yourself of love, your ability to manifest an abundant life becomes affected. It is only when you become present to your suffering that you begin to realize that you are the mystery that you have been hoping to solve. All external search ceases in favor of investigating from within. Eventually, you will realize that everything that has surfaced is to help you increase your capacity for love.

You learn that every moment represents a chance for renewal. In fact, every moment is a choice between love and fear. And hence, you can make the choice of love. In practical terms, your task is to release fear. You learn that to be human is to give up your fears of being vulnerable, looking imperfect and not being good enough. When you do so, you strip away the layers that cover the ultimate truth of your soul. You experience the essence of love – that which you already are.

Remove fear in your mind and reawaken to the love in your heart. To do so requires an investigation into your negative self-talk and releasing the emotions, that have bolted your heart. The shift is essentially a continuum that takes you from dark to light, from confusion to clarity, from being asleep to being awakened, and from being numbed to feeling totally alive. From a self-love starver, you transmute into the gold of who you are through the process of alchemy. You become a love luminary. In fact, the path towards integration is what I have shared in my book, Abundance Alchemy: Journey of Gold.

Self-love involves getting in touch with your breath. Your heart moves according to your in- and out-breath. The breath represents the start and end of life. With inhalation, your heart expands in capacity. You are receiving from the universe. With exhalation, your heart contracts in capacity. You are giving back to the universe. The receiving-giving cycle of life is no different from the receiving-giving cycle of love. You receive love from yourself and everyone else, and you also give love back in return. Just like life, love needs to circulate. Life is love. And love is life.

By making the decision to love yourself, you are really saying that you want to come alive. You accept that you are responsible for the outcomes that you experience in your life and would like yourself to shine from living a fulfilling life. You want to celebrate every part of being you. Hence you do not hold yourself back but become willing to explore your unlimited potential.

The ultimate secret to manifesting a full life is first found through self-love. Self-love is the heart of your spiritual journey on Earth. It gets built upon with each affirmation of love as your choice in presenting situations. You are repeatedly called to affirm "I am lovable", "I am good enough" and "I am worthy and deserving". Through self-love, you come to know your physical being as the conscious expression of infinite source. By aligning yourself with authentic purpose, you naturally bring who you really are forward in your life and live to your highest potential.

Self-love is having the freedom to be yourself, without experiencing the need to judge, censor or lie. There is no cloak that you are hiding under. You are your basic nature. You are free to be you. You are free from fear. Your body will turn to ashes one day but love, the essence of who you are, lives forever.

Eventually, you feel a love not only for yourself but also, in extension to all others. Because you can see how beautiful you are – even with all your imperfections, you also awaken to the beauty of everything that is external. Not only do you experience peace, joy, kindness, forgiveness, compassion, respect and trust on the inside, you also experience these qualities on the outside and in every facet of existence.

The shift in consciousness that happens to you in self-love results in the shift in consciousness in the entire universe. Pure love from your heart reaches and touches every being in the cosmos. It is a heart that beats to the same rhythm of the heart of the universe. Love seals the experience of oneness in a previously separate world. From the inside, you align yourself closer with Source. On the outside, love unites hearts and fosters togetherness. And from the outside, love flows back to you.

Your presence creates a positive effect on others. They become drawn to your inner light. Your radiance comes from a deep inner awareness of who you are. The light from self-awareness dissolves the darkness from fear. If a miracle is possible for you, it can be possible for them too. Hence, anyone is likely to be inspired by your very example and become shining beacons themselves. Loving yourself, thus, creates a rippling effect in consciousness. There will be less starving of love in the world.

Love is meaning, movement and magic. Love transforms ordinary and dull relationships, events and things into experiences that are vibrant, purposeful and beautiful. Through embracing the self, love flows freely and fully; like a running river of pure energized water. With love living through your soul, you gain a glimpse into the eternal soul of the universe. It is love living into itself. Meeting yourself at the center, you reclaim your divinity. Through your being, you awaken into the totality of all there-is. Through self-love, you are led spiritually home.

Bibliography

A Course in Miracles. Foundation for Inner Peace, CA, 2007.

Brené Brown. *The Gifts of Imperfection.* Center City, MN: Hazelden, 2010.

Daphne Rose Kingma. *Loving Yourself: Four Steps to a Happier You.* CA, Conari Press, 2004.

Deepak Chopra. *Reinventing the Body, Resurrecting the Soul.* Ebury Publishing, United States, 2009.

Don Miguel Ruiz. *The Mastery of Love: A Practical Guide to the Art of Relationship.* Amber-Allen Publishing, CA, 1999.

Don Richard Riso and Russ Hudson. *The Wisdom of the Enneagram.* New York, Batam Books, 1999.

Eckhart Tolle. *A New Earth: Awakening to Your Life Purpose.* Penguin Group, London, 2005.

Louis Hay. *You can Heal Your Life.* United States, Hay House, 1984.

Marianne Williamson. *A Return to Love: Reflections on the Principles of a Course in Miracles.* Harper Collins Publishers 1993.

Masaru Emoto. *The Hidden Messages in Water.* Beyond Words Publishing, Oregon, 2004.

Masaru Emoto. *The True Power of Water.* Beyond Words Publishing, Oregon, 2004.

Sharon Wegscheider-Cruse. *Learning to Love Yourself: Finding Your Self-Worth.* Communications Inc, FL, 1987.

Stephanie Dowrick. *Creative Journal Writing.* Penguin Group, United States, 2009.

Thich Nhat Hanh. *Teachings on Love.* Parallax Press, CA, 2007.

About The Author

Evelyn Lim is the author of the book "Abundance Alchemy: Journey of Gold". She is also co-author to "Adventures in Manifesting: Success and Spirituality" together with other well-known authors such as Dr Joe Vitale and Dr Fred Alan Wolf (teachers from "The Secret" movie), and Dr Brian Tracy. Professionally, she is a life coach, intuitive consultant and vision board counselor from Singapore.

Evelyn is passionate about creating greater self-love awareness. She enjoys sharing with others the message: "Change begins with you. Be a luminary of love and light." Evelyn intends to live her best possible life, and by doing so, inspire others to do the same. She is dedicated to doing work as a creative expression of who she is. She now assists her clients and readers with shifting to higher vibrational energy states.

Evelyn offers practical life tips, compelling insights, and inspiring stories on her website. Her website draws thousands of readers from around the world every month. To read more about her or to gain free access to her articles, please visit http://www.AbundanceTapestry.com.